PRESENTED TO:

_____

FROM:

_____

DATE:

_____

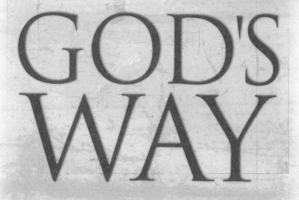

TEENS

LIVING THE ULTIMATE CHALLENGE...

GOD'S WAY

WS

WHITE STONE BOOKS
LAKELAND, FLORIDA

07 06 05 04 03 02 01   10 9 8 7 6 5 4 3 2 1

Teens—Living the Ultimate Challenge...God's Way
ISBN 1-59379-008-2
Copyright © 2003 John M. Thurber
Thurber Creative Services, Inc.
Tulsa, Oklahoma

Editorial Development and Literary Representation by
Mark Gilroy Communications, Inc.
6528 E. 101st Street, Suite 416
Tulsa, Oklahoma 74133-6754

Editorial Manager: Christy Sterner

Published by White Stone Books, Inc.
P.O. Box 2835
Lakeland, Florida 33806

INTRODUCTION

He has made His wonderful works to be remembered.

PSALM 111:4 NKJV

God is at work today in the lives of young people all around the world—revealing His purpose, demonstrating His awesome power, and transforming lives into incredible futures.

Are you looking for answers to the many questions you deal with as a teen?

Perhaps you are face-to-face with pressures at school or with friends, a challenging situation in your home, or even uncertainties about your future. Maybe you simply need a little inspiration to strengthen your heart.

God's Way for Teens is filled with true stories that reveal powerful insights from teens experiencing the same challenges as you.

Discover the incredible potential and excellence God has appointed for your life as you continue on your life's journey—and seek to achieve what it truly means to live...*God's Way.*

CONTENTS

THE DAY THE CHEERING STOPPED

JOHN C. STEWART

(as told to Gloria Cassity Stargel; names in this story have been changed)

**There is rejoicing in the presence of the angels
of God over one sinner who repents.**

LUKE 15:10 NIV

It happened on a cold day in January, midway through my senior year in high school. I tossed my books into the locker and reached for my black and gold Cougar jacket. From down the corridor, a friend called out, "Good luck, Johnny. I hope you get the school you want!"

Playing football was more than a game to me. It was my *life*. So the world looked pretty wonderful as I headed up the hill toward the gym to learn which college wanted me on its team.

How I counted on the scholarship—I had for years! It held my only hope for higher education. My dad, an alcoholic, had left

9

home long ago, and Mom worked two jobs just to keep seven children fed. I even held down part-time jobs to help out.

But I wasn't worried. I had the grades I needed. And ever since elementary school, I had lived and breathed football. It was my entire identity.

Growing up in a little southern town where football is king, my skills on the field made me a big man in the community as well as on my high-school campus. I pictured myself right up there on a pedestal—where most people would have placed me.

Everyone helped to pump up my ego. The local newspaper mentioned me in write-ups; at football games exuberant cheerleaders yelled out my name; people constantly made comments like, "You can do it, Johnny. You can go all the way to professional football!" And I ate it up. In a way, it made up for my not having a dad to encourage me along the way.

Hurrying to the gym that day, I recalled all those football games—and all those *injuries!* I never had let any of them slow me down for long—not the broken back or the messed-up shoulders and knees—I just gritted my teeth and played right through the agony. I *had* to.

And now came the reward. A good future would be worth the price I had paid. So with a confident grin on my face, I sauntered into Coach Stone's office.

Coach sat behind his desk, the papers from my file spread before him. Our three other coaches sat around the room. No doubt about it, this lineup signaled a momentous occasion.

"Have a seat, Johnny," Coach motioned to the chair beside his desk.

"Johnny," he started, "you've worked really hard. You've done a good job for us. A couple of colleges want to make you an offer."

Something about his tone made me nervous. I shifted my sitting position.

"But, Johnny," he said, holding my medical records in his hands, "Doctor Kendley can't recommend you for college football. Johnny, one more bad hit, and you could be paralyzed for life. We can't risk it."

A long silence followed. Then Coach Stone's eyes met mine. "I'm sorry, Johnny. There will be no scholarship."

No scholarship?! The blow hit me like a 300-pound linebacker slamming against my chest. Somehow I got out of that office. I could not seem to understand that they were thinking of my welfare. Instead, all I could think was, *You're not good enough, you're not good enough, you're not good enough.*

For *me*, the cheering stopped. Without the cheering, I was nothing. And without college, I would *stay* a nothing.

After that, I just gave up. And in so doing, I lost my grip on life.

At first, I settled for beer and marijuana. Soon I got into the hard stuff: acid, PCP, heroin, cocaine—I tried them all. By the time graduation rolled around, it was a wonder I even made it through the ceremonies.

Several older friends tried to talk to me about God. Yet even though I had grown up in church, had even served as an altar boy, I couldn't grasp the fact that God had anything to do with my present situation.

A couple of buddies and I decided to hit the road. We had no money and no goal. Along the way, we got into stealing gas to keep us going. When we got hungry enough, we picked up some odd jobs. No matter how little food we had, we always managed to get more drugs.

My anger continued to build. It wasn't long until I got into a bad fight and landed in jail thousands of miles from home. It caused me to take a good look at myself and see how low I had sunk. *God,* I prayed for the first time in years, *please help me. I'm lost, and I can't find my way back.*

I didn't hear an immediate answer. Nor did I clean up my act. We *did* head toward home, but the old car had had enough. It quit.

I went into a garage, hoping to get some cheap parts. *Maybe I can patch her up enough to get us home,* I thought. I was tired, hungry, dirty—and very much under the influence. Yet a man there extended a hand of friendship. He even took us to supper. After we were fed, Mr. Brown called me aside, "Son," he said, "you don't have to live like this. You can be somebody if only you'll try. God will help you. Remember, He loves you. And so do I."

I was buffaloed. He seemed to care about me. And he had called me "Son." It had been a long, long time since a man had called me "Son."

That night, in my sleeping bag, I gazed up at the star-filled Texas night. The sky looked so close, I thought maybe I could reach up and touch it. And once again, I tried to pray. *Lord, I am so tired. If You'll have me, I'm ready to come back to You.*

In my heart, I heard God answer, *I'm here. Come on back, Son. I'm here.* He called me "Son," just like Mr. Brown had. I liked that.

On the road again, I got to thinking: *If Mr. Brown, a complete stranger, thinks I can make something of myself, maybe I can.*

I didn't straighten out all at once. But at least I started trying. And God kept sending people to help me. Like Susan. In September, this cute young thing—a casual friend from high school—came up to me at a football game, of all places. She kissed me on the cheek and said, "Welcome home, Johnny."

The day she said, "Johnny, if you keep doing drugs, I can't date you anymore," was the day I quit them for good.

Susan and I married, and today we have three beautiful children. We're active in our local church and operate a successful business. I can tell you it means the world to me to have earned the respect of my community.

All these years later, I still can feel the sting of that day—the day the cheering stopped. The hurt doesn't linger though, as I've learned I can live without the cheers of a human crowd. After all, I have a caring Heavenly Father who calls me "Son." And I *do* have a cheering section—a Heavenly one. Check out this Bible verse I discovered: "There is rejoicing in the presence of the angels of God over one sinner who repents " (Luke 15:10 NIV).

How about that?

Angels! Cheering for *ME!*

I like that.

THE UNEXPECTED MIRACLE

AMY ALLEN

(as told to Esther M. Bailey)

To him who is able to do immeasurably more than all we ask or imagine...to him be glory...in Christ Jesus.

EPHESIANS 3:20-21 NIV

Wow! God really did it up big! It had never entered my mind to ask Him for a full-tuition scholarship to college, but when I read the letter, I felt like God had carved my name on His latest miracle.

At the same time, I realized the price that had been paid for my joy. The Bible college was offering the scholarship in honor of the ministry of a man I had called Grandpa before he died, and Grandma Frick had chosen me to receive the memorial grant. Even in death Grandpa was there for me as he had been in life.

Ever since I can remember, Grandma and Grandpa Frick were part of my life. My real grandparents lived in different cities, but the Fricks were always nearby. They were my Christian role models as well as my adopted grandparents.

I looked back at what God had already done for me and wondered what He had in store for my future.

Growing up in the church, I had always done Christian things. I asked Jesus to come into my heart as soon as I knew I should. It wasn't until I was in the eighth grade that I realized I needed something more. I was really down on myself—to the point that I even considered suicide. *What do I have to live for?* I kept asking myself. *I'm ugly, and I'm tired of being called a "Jesus freak" or a "church girl."*

When my dad sensed that something was terribly wrong, we had a talk. Dad listened and then told me, "Name some things you *do* like."

I answered with the first things that popped into my mind: "Sunsets...dolphins."

"Amy, you know that if you died today you could never see another sunset. You'd never see the dolphins that you've always wanted to see." Dad reminded me that life is good even during the toughest of times, and he pointed out the words of Scripture. The verse that made the greatest impression on me was Psalm 139:14 NIV: "I praise you because I am fearfully and wonderfully made." I didn't need to feel bad about myself because God "doesn't make trash."

For the first time I realized how much I needed Christ to walk with me every day of my life. I wanted to serve God with all of my heart, all of my mind, and all of my soul so that I would be totally focused on Him.

My struggles didn't go away, but I had Someone to share them with. During my freshman year of high school, the school seemed so big that I just sort of faded into the background. I didn't do the kind of stuff other kids were doing; so I didn't fit in with the crowd. My youth group at church was what kept me going.

I moved several times during the early part of high school. Every time I moved, the kids would invite me to a party. I always explained, "No, I don't drink," and then they would ask me why. When I said, "I'm a Christian," that cooled almost all possible friendships.

During my last two years of high school, I started incorporating my Christian witness into my school papers. In English, we were asked to write about the most important thing in life. I wrote about my relationship with God. Teachers sometimes cause trouble for kids who stand up for God, but my teachers didn't.

Finally, guys started asking me out—gorgeous guys that all the girls dreamed over. But I turned them down because I knew they weren't right for me.

I stood true to my standards all through high school, but it would have been so easy to fall into a trap. I had a lot of lonely nights because I wanted to go to parties and go out with guys. A lot of times I wanted to give up and say, *Forget it. This Christian thing is too much work.* Thank God that I didn't!

I dated a few guys in my youth group at church. Most of the dates I went on were casual, but I did have a few serious relationships. We did a lot of things with groups because we didn't want to let down our guard.

One of my biggest struggles came right after high school graduation. Most everyone who was close to me moved away—including my boyfriend and several good friends. Even my sister was gone for a good part of the summer. I was frustrated about college. I knew that I wanted to make something of myself. For the previous two years I had worked at Dairy Queen, and I knew I didn't want to do *that* the rest of my life! Bible college was too far away and cost too much; so I figured I'd just go to a community college.

Then the scholarship came, and I was totally amazed. It was as though God had opened the door and shoved me right through! I could see how He had prepared me to leave home by slowly pulling my friends away and causing me to rely on Him. During my time alone, I had learned to depend upon God instead of people. And I treasured my time with Him more than anything else.

College with Christian friends will be great. I suppose I'll have struggles there too, but I'm too excited to get concerned about that right now. Being "a good girl" hasn't always been easy; in fact, it's been hard at times. But without a doubt it's been worth it. I now walk with a lot of self-confidence and my head held high. I'm proud to be where I am. When I get discouraged, I'll just hang in there and remember that God has always been there for me and will continue to always be there.

THE DAY LISA LOST

MICHAEL T. POWERS

"Not so with you. Instead whoever wants to become great among you must be your servant, and whoever wants to be first must be your slave."

MATTHEW 20:26-27 NIV

I admire athletes! Don't get me wrong. I'm not talking about the many professional athletes of today who have developed a "me first" attitude, after being raised in a "win at all cost" generation, where role models are severely lacking and too many of the headlines that capture our attention are of those athletes who are in trouble. No, I am talking about high-school sports, where lessons of life are still being learned and where athletes still compete for the love of the game and their teammates.

I know some of you are thinking, *The high-school athletes of today are just as bad!* And you would be partially right. The "me first" attitude is trickling down into more and more high-school and junior-high athletes.

In the midst of all this, however, is a young lady from Wisconsin.

I first met Lisa on the volleyball court as she played for a rival conference high school. Many times I was on the opposing sidelines as a coach and could only watch in awe at her athleticism: She had the speed of a cheetah, the mental toughness of a veteran, and a thirty-two-inch vertical jump! She possessed skills unheard of for a high-school student—and she was only a sophomore!

At the beginning of her junior year, I was fortunate enough to coach Lisa on a USA Junior Olympic volleyball team, and it was during the next two years that my wife and I grew to love and respect her, not just for her many athletic abilities, but for her unselfishness and humility—despite the many honors that were bestowed on her. Besides being one of the most coachable athletes I've ever known, she was the epitome of a team player.

If anyone had earned a right to be cocky and proud of herself, it was Lisa. Besides being one of the best volleyball and basketball players in the state, she became a legend in track and field. How good was she? She attended sixty-four straight conference meets and never lost in any event she entered. She made trips to the state finals all four years she was in high school and came away with six state titles. Many times she was her team's lone representative at the state competition, and she would single-handedly place her high school as high as third place.

While she excelled in the triple jump, the long jump, and the 100- and 200-meter dashes, there were times when her coach needed her to fill in for other events. One particular day he asked her to run the 300-meter hurdles. She had never competed in that event before, but the coach needed her that day for the good of the team. How did she do? She not only won, but she set the school record in the first and only time she competed in the event!

Despite all of these achievements, there was one particular track meet during Lisa's junior year in which she showed me what is truly good about sports these days.

It was a non-conference meet late in the year and Lisa's coach entered her in the 1600-meter race. As before, Lisa had never competed in this event and was puzzled as to why she had been entered.

Lisa easily outdistanced the competition, but on the last lap, she "seemed" to grow "tired." Two athletes from the other team passed her, and then so did Jane, Lisa's teammate. Lisa stayed just behind her teammate and crossed the finish line at her heels.

Lisa had lost an event for the first time in her track career.

It wasn't until later that I learned the rest of the story.

You see, athletes in Lisa's track program needed to earn a set number of points in order to earn a varsity letter. Lisa knew that Jane, who was a senior, needed to finish at least third to earn a letter for the first time. Lisa also knew that the two athletes on the other team were most likely going to beat Jane in the event. Jane would have been a lock for third—until the coach entered Lisa in the race.

After four years of working hard, Jane finally received her first varsity letter. And Lisa? She had a smile on her face, even when she lost.

On that day, she earned my respect and admiration and in my mind, solidified herself as the role model this generation sorely needs.

Sometimes you can lose and still win.

SWEET SIXTEEN

SHELLY TEEMS JOHNSON

(as told to Gloria Cassity Stargel)

Children, obey your parents....If you honor your father and mother, yours will be a long life, full of blessing.

EPHESIANS 6:1,3 TLB

"Hurry and get dressed, Shelly," Mom's overly-cheerful voice penetrated the closed door to my room. "The sun's shining. Let's go riding!"

Mom knew good and well that I was on the phone with my boyfriend. The last thing in the world I wanted to do on that Sunday afternoon was go horseback riding with my mother. Yet I dared not argue back, not after our blowup the night before. *I'm sixteen years old, for crying out loud!* I seethed. *Why can't she just stay out of my life?*

Sometimes, I *hated* my mother. I desperately wanted her to give me a little space. She sponsored my cheerleader squad. She came to every one of my volleyball and softball games. She even

25

taught at my school. Wherever I went, she was there! As if that weren't bad enough, she was always ordering me around. Even my friends commented about it.

When I was little, I *liked* it when Mom was protective, when she got involved in my activities. But now I wanted more independence, a chance to make my own mistakes.

The truth is, despite Mom's constant surveillance, I managed to break most of the rules at our private Christian school. And the more I rebelled, the more Mom clamped down. The more she clamped down, the more I rebelled.

Take the night before, for example, when we had the blowup. Okay, so I *was* a few minutes late coming in. Well, maybe it was more like an *hour* late. Anyway, just as I expected, Mom followed me into my room. "Where were you all this time, Shelly? I worry about you when you're late. *Anything* could have happened! Why didn't you call me?" On and on and on she went.

As usual Mom threw in a little scripture for good measure, as if she didn't already drill me on memory verses at our breakfast table *every morning of the week!* "Remember, Shelly," she'd said that night, "the Bible says, 'Children, obey your parents.... If you honor your father and mother, yours will be a long life, full of blessing.'" Then she added, "Shelly, your life has just been shortened by one day!"

"Mom," I yelled, "will you just leave me alone!" When she finally left, I slammed the door behind her.

Now today she was pretending that nothing had happened, trying to make us look like the ideal loving family of her dreams. Meanwhile, after hanging up the telephone, I was sitting there thinking, *What is all this horseback-riding business? Mom isn't even a horse person! She just wants to know what I'm doing every minute.*

Half-heartedly, I pulled on my riding boots, then stomped over to the dresser. Reaching for a comb, my hand brushed against the necklace Mom had given me for my last birthday. *I'd better wear this or she'll ask where it is.* Reluctantly, I fastened the silver chain around my neck and straightened the pendant—the silver outline of a heart with its message, in script, suspended inside: "Sweet Sixteen." *Yeah, sure, Mom.*

By the time I got to the barn, Dad had already saddled Miss Char-Deck—we usually called her Charcey. Mom was swinging into the saddle. "Mom, *what* are you doing?" I shrieked. "You've never ridden Charcey before! She's a *big* horse." *I cannot believe this woman!* I thought. *She'll do anything to be part of my life. And I just want her out of it!*

While Dad was bridling the Arabian named Babe, Mom discovered her stirrups were too long. Before Dad could turn around to adjust them, Charcey charged away at full gallop.

Scared and inexperienced, Mom had probably reacted by doing all the wrong things. Whatever the reason, Charcey was out of control. Never had I seen that horse run so fast, her mane and tail flying in the wind! It was as though she had to show off what a quarterhorse is bred to do: win short-distance races. And with every stride of her powerful haunches, she gained speed.

I watched, horrified, as Charcey's hooves beat at the earth, faster and faster—like something possessed, a thousand pounds of straining muscle thundering across the pasture.

With lightning speed, Charcey reached a corner of the pasture fence—a place of decision. Should she jump? *No. Too high with a ditch on the other side.* Her other choice? *Make a ninety-degree turn.* Charcey turned. Mom flew high into the air, crashed through a barbed-wire fence, and landed on the sun-parched ground. THUD.

Then—*nothing!* Except for Charcey's hoof beats as she tore back to the barn.

Dear God! No! No! This can't be happening! I sprinted across the pasture, outrunning Dad on the Arabian. "Mom! Mom!" *Please, God, don't let her be dead! I didn't mean it, God. I don't really want her out of my life! Please!*

The barbed wire was holding her in an almost kneeling position. Her right wrist and hand dangled the wrong way, her neck and head were turned as if broken, and blood oozed from gashes on her back. *Is she breathing? Please, God, she thinks I don't love her!* "Mom?"

After what seemed like an eternity, I heard a moan—then a weak, "I'm okay, Shelly."

"Mom! Oh, Mom! I didn't mean to be so hateful. I *do* love you, Mom!" Ever so carefully, I began untangling her hair from the barbed wire, barely able to see through my tears. "Oh, Mama, I'm so sorry. I'm so sorry."

"I know, Shelly," Mom somehow managed, while I made one last tug on her now-shredded pink sweater and freed her from the wire.

"We've got to get you to the hospital," Dad said, jumping back astride Babe and turning her toward the barn. "I'll call an ambulance."

"No," Mom said, and because she was a nurse, we listened. "You can take me in the van."

It wasn't easy, but we did it. Dad barreled down the highway, all the while trying to raise a police escort on the two-way radio. Meanwhile, I did what Mom had taught me—I quoted Scripture, the first one that popped into my head. "Rejoice in the Lord always," I said, close to her ear, "and again I say rejoice." For *once,* I must have done the right thing. Because Mom, even in all her pain, started quoting Scripture, one verse after another, all the way to the hospital.

Mom spent most of the next three months in a wheelchair, and during that time the two of us did a lot of talking. "Mom," I told her, "I know I act a lot like Charcey did that day of the accident. I just want to charge through life without being held back, not missing anything."

"Yes, Shelly, and I always want to be in control, to make sure things go right. To protect you from getting hurt."

We decided because we were very different, we'd probably *always* clash over one thing or another.

But we agreed on something else too. That we loved each other, no matter what.

Still, I felt a need to do something more to make things right. One day at school I asked permission to say a few words at our chapel service.

Standing on stage behind the microphone, I took a deep breath and started. To the other students, to the faculty, and especially to Mom who sat in the back of the room in her wheelchair, I said, "I want to apologize for all the mistakes I've made this year, mistakes that have hurt others. Worst of all, they have hurt my mom."

I told them how hateful I had been to my mother. How I had yelled at her to stay out of my life. Then I told them about Mom's accident. About how at the thought of losing her, I realized that she is my very best friend. That she wanted only what is best for me. "Please, you guys," I begged my fellow students, "tell your mother you love her. Don't wait until it's too late, like I almost did."

I looked back at Mom who was beaming, while dabbing at her eyes with a tissue. "Mom," I said, voice quivering, "I ask you to forgive me. I ask *God* to forgive me."

As if on cue, one of Mom's Bible verses popped into my head. "If we confess our sins, he is faithful and just to forgive us our sins...." *Thank You, God, for believing in me, even when I disappoint You over and over.*

Just like Mom! I realized in a flash of insight. Instinctively, I reached up and caressed the silver pendant at my neck. My fingers traced the intricate lettering, "Sweet Sixteen." *Sixteen? Yes. Sweet? Hardly! But I will try, Mom,* I smiled through my tears. *I will try.*

Leaving the platform, suddenly I became aware of a new feeling—one I'd never really felt before. A realization in my heart that seemed to say, *It's okay, Shelly, to let your mom into your life.*

Even when you're sweet sixteen.

GOD TOOK ME IN

KEN FREEMAN

My father and mother walked out and left me,

but God took me in.

PSALM 27:10 THE MESSAGE

None of the stepfathers and strangers who meandered through my life filled the simple need I had for a father. I hungered for someone who would teach me how to throw a ball, play catch with me, take me fishing, show me how to build a campfire, read me a bedtime story, and reassure me with a hug. I needed a father to show affection for my mother, so I could know the security of a stable, loving home. I needed someone who would work hard, so I could have adequate physical nourishment and provision. Most importantly, I needed a father to demonstrate responsibility, so I would know how to act like a man.

I didn't have any of those things from my father. I don't know exactly when he left. One day I just realized he was gone. When

I asked Mom where Dad was, she growled, "He's gone, and he ain't comin' back." Oh, how I missed Dad! None of my nine stepfathers could fill the void—not even the stepfather who stayed around the longest.

This stepfather even played a little baseball with me, although I was usually such an emotional bundle of nerves that I struggled to enjoy it. I placed intense pressure on myself to perform. I thought if I did well, others would like me and want to be my friend. I even managed to make a Little League team one summer.

For years I thought all men were idiots and worthless drunks. The only male role models I had ever known were shiftless, dishonest vagabonds whose primary joy in life was winning a poker hand. Though I detested these men, unfortunately, I was on the road to becoming just like them. Taking up smoking and drinking at the age of ten, I learned how to lie, cheat, and steal with the skill of a seasoned, small-time jailbird.

This kind of influence stirred an inward anger that fueled my disrespect for rules and a contempt for anyone in authority. I hated my father because he wasn't around. And I hated the other men who drifted in and out of our lives. After my parents divorced, every man Mom married was someone she met in a tavern. I don't know if any of them ever held steady jobs because they usually walked around with hangovers. I greeted each new stepfather with hope, but it didn't take long before I came to despise the fact that instead of one drunk parent at home, there were two, which doubled the intensity of the fighting and swearing.

I learned to drive at thirteen because of my parents' irresponsible behavior. We were on our way home one night when one of my stepfathers suddenly slumped over the wheel. Reaching from the backseat, I frantically shook him by the shoulders. Startled, he smacked the brakes and jerked the car off to the side of the road. Finally, he got out the door, stumbled, and fell on the pavement. After wavering to his feet, he climbed into the backseat. I crawled up front and drove us home, my hands shaking as I strained to see over the wheel.

All of this happened in the fifties and sixties, that supposedly blissful era that spawned such feel-good television shows as *Leave It to Beaver, Father Knows Best, Dennis the Menace,* and *The Andy Griffith Show.* To this day I love watching the reruns, especially of Andy Griffith. Andy was a great father and Opie always called him "Pa." Andy represented the father I had wanted so badly.

I often imagined how great it would be to have a dad who came home sober and spent time with his family. But most of the time I just watched television and daydreamed about a true family. This reverie provided a tidbit of imaginary security.

Blocking out reality, I would muster enough strength to make it through another day, hoping that someday I would lead a normal life.

But I didn't give myself much hope and neither did anyone else.

Then I met Jeff.

Jeff McGowan was a defensive lineman on the high-school football team. We called him Cowboy because he wasn't afraid of anything or anybody—even though at only six feet tall and less than two hundred pounds, he wasn't all that big. He wasn't conceited over his status as a football star. Everyone liked Jeff, who was president of the Christian club at school. Like me, he came from a broken home, but he didn't seem soured by his past. That impressed me. He had a beautiful way of relating to other people. I wanted to be more like Jeff, but I just didn't know how.

Jeff kept inviting me to church, and each time I invented a creative excuse not to go. After several rejections, Jeff told me that an evangelist named Freddie Gage was coming to his church. To persuade me to come, he mentioned that they were serving pizza and that some of the girls I liked would be there. As usual, I made a lame excuse.

To my surprise, however, Jeff showed up at my front door later that day with a resolute look on his face.

"Dude, you're goin'," he proclaimed.

I thought a moment. He was bigger than I was. I didn't mind getting some free pizza. It was a chance to meet a few babes.

"Okay," I nodded.

As we drove downtown to the church, I plotted my escape. As soon as I had a chance to eat, I would sneak out the back door. When we arrived, I felt a twinge of nervousness. The only time I had been inside a church before was to steal something or to set wastebaskets on fire. I didn't really know anything about God, and I wondered if my former pranks would come back to haunt me. I felt like an invader in the enemy's camp.

In spite of my cigarette-soaked, repulsive-smelling clothing, nobody shunned me. I was pleasantly surprised by everyone's friendliness.

Then, I found out the pizza would be served after the service, not before. And Jeff didn't intend to give me a chance to dart out early. He followed me around like a hawk before suggesting we go inside the sanctuary and find a seat. *All right,* I told myself, *I'll get through this, meet some people, and then never do this thing again.*

I followed Jeff as he walked up to the front, onto the stage, and into the choir section! At first, I thought it was a joke. But everyone in the choir hugged me and treated me like an old friend. Soon the music started, transforming me into a choir member. I sang some familiar hymns, such as "Amazing Grace." When I didn't know a song, I stuck my head behind the book or mouthed the words silently until I picked up the tune.

When the music stopped, I analyzed the situation. Looking down at the bottom of the first page of the hymnal and seeing that the song had been written in 1732, I almost burst into laughter. These oddballs were singing songs nearly 250 years old!

The music wasn't the only thing I found amusing. When it started and the director stood up, dramatically waving his arms, I thought he was having back spasms. These folks were definitely weird. Especially those who hugged me and said, "We love you, brother!" *I don't even know who your mom is,* I thought, *so how did I become your brother?* Then the evangelist came onstage.

At first I didn't take Freddie Gage seriously, despite his dramatic opening line: "All my friends are dead." Gage went on to describe how he grew up on the streets of Houston, abusing drugs and running with a gang. Because he had turned his life over to God, he said, he was the only gang member who had survived to age twenty-five. After God turned his life around, Gage had gone back to the bars, but now he stood on pool tables to preach.

"Some of you have been drinking, doing drugs, and messing up your life," he said, a remark that startled me. *How did he know what I'd been doing?*

I thought Jeff had somehow slipped out before the service and told the evangelist all about me before he went onstage. And now, there he was, spilling my secrets to the whole church!

Then, the congregation got me laughing again, by shouting "Amen!"

Yet as he talked, I could see that he really believed what he was saying. His passion and intensity in his belief in God was reflected in his eyes. I thought, *If someone is this serious about God and could believe in Him that strongly, maybe I should listen.* I quit thinking about the petty things that had distracted me and started paying attention to this fiery evangelist.

"God's got a purpose for your life," he pointed out. My heart thumped. *A purpose? For me?* "God loves everybody," he continued. "There's nothing you've done or could do that would keep God from loving you. But you've got to receive Him and believe in Him.

I thought about the times I had tried to commit suicide or daydreamed about killing myself. My mind wandered back over all the drugs, drinking, crime, and shattered dreams that had dominated my life. Maybe there *was* an answer—a way out of this mess. Maybe *God* was the answer. Maybe this evangelist wasn't such a goofball. After all, he had come from the streets of Houston. If he could turn his life around, maybe I could too.

I began to weep as the evangelist neared the end of his message. All the emotional garbage of the past surfaced and melted my heart. I may have hardened myself on the outside, but inside I knew the truth: I was hurting. I wanted relief from the pain. Still, there was a fierce tug-of-war going on inside me. This evangelist's message had touched me, but I wasn't too sure of what was happening. When he asked everyone to bow their heads, I only half-bowed mine. I was determined to keep an eye on things.

"If you'd like to have what I have, stand up," he said.

Without thinking or realizing what I was doing, I stood. For the first time in my life, I didn't care what anyone else thought. When Gage invited those who had stood up to walk to the altar where he was standing, I obeyed.

"Son, do you know you're a sinner?" he asked. The first thing I wanted to say was, "I'm not your son." Instead, I shook my head and said, "Sir, I don't know what I am. All I know is my mom wants me dead. She thinks I came from hell, and I haven't seen my dad in more than a dozen years. I don't have a real family, and I've got a stepdad whose a drunk. I've tried suicide.

That's all I know. If this Jesus can make my life better, then I want to know Him."

He guaranteed me Christ could do that.

"Will this Jesus ever leave me?" I asked.

"You might turn your back on Him, but He will never turn His back on you."

That convinced me. At his urging, we knelt to pray. I would have done anything he asked, from turning cartwheels to performing jumping jacks. I trusted this guy and I wanted what he had.

At that moment God touched and transformed my life.

When I knelt to pray with that evangelist, God saw my hungering faith, and I accepted His free gift of salvation by faith in His Son, Jesus Christ.

Looking back, I am thankful for the friendship of a school friend...who reached out to me. But most of all to God, who reached all the way down to a messed-up sixteen-year-old in the choir loft and gave me a brand-new life—one that still amazes, thrills, and satisfies me.

POSTCARDS FROM MY SON

CHARLIE "TREMENDOUS" JONES

Jesus increased in wisdom and stature,

and in favour with God and man.

LUKE 2:52

When my son was fourteen, I said, "Jerry, do you want to have a car when you're sixteen?" "Yes." "Do you want me to help you buy that car?" "Yes sir, Dad." "Alright, Son, we're going to do it, but the free ride's over. No more allowance. Instead, I'm going to give you a way to make a lot of money.

"Here is the deal. I am going to pick out books for you to read. There will be motivational books, history books, inspirational books; every time I give you a book, you give me a book report. Every time I get a book report, I'll put money in your car fund. Another book report—more money in the car fund. In two years if you read in style, you'll drive in style. But if you read like a bum, you're going to drive like a bum."

Overnight my son developed a fantastic hunger for reading! The first book I had him read was Dale Carnegie's *How to Win Friends and Influence People*. The first day he came down and said, "Dad, there's a whole chapter in here on smiling and shaking hands!" And then he shook my hand and smiled at me.

Next I had him read a book about Joshua in the Old Testament and discouragement. As we were going to Sunday school the next week, I asked, "Jerry, how are you getting along with Joshua?" He said, "Dad!" And he playfully hit my leg. Imagine that, he hit my leg! Then he said, "Everybody ought to read that book!" That was a sign he was beginning to think about somebody other than himself.

Well, Jerry read twenty-two books. Did he buy a car? No. He kept the money and used my car and my gas! But it was worth it.

After he went off to college, he began to write me a "Dear Dad" postcard every day for four years. And I could tell that he was thinking thoughts I never dreamed a young person could think. Here's what a few of the postcards said:

"Dear Dad, It's tremendous to be able to know that when you are in a slump, just as a baseball player will break out in time, so will you break out of yours. Yes, time really cures things. Like you said, you don't lose any problems, you just get bigger and better ones, tremendous ones. Tremendously too. Jerry"

"Dear Dad, Just started reading *A Hundred Great Lives.* Thanks for what you said in the front. The part that every great man never sought to be great. He just followed the vision he had and did what had to be done. Love, Jerry."

"Dad, I just got done typing up little quotes out of the Bible, so everywhere I look, I see them. When people ask me what they are, I tell them they are pinups. Tremendously."

"Dad, I am more convinced than ever that you can do anything you want to. You can beat anyone at anything just by working hard. Handicaps don't mean anything. Because often people that don't have them have a bad attitude and don't want to work."

"Dad, nothing new. Just the same old exciting thought that we can know God personally and forever in this amazing life."

"Dad, when you're behind two papers in the fourth quarter and you're exhausted from the game, you have to make up a set of downs in order to stay in the game. When you get up to the line and you see two, 250-pound tests staring you in the face, it sure is exciting to wait and find out what play the Lord will call next."

A proper diet is good for your body, and good books are good for your mind. So, read, read, read!

Your life will be determined by the people you associate with and the books you read. You will come to love many people you will meet in books. Read biographies, autobiographies, and books on history. Books will provide many of the friends, mentors, role models, and heroes you will need in life. Biographies will help you see that there is nothing that can happen to you that wasn't experienced by many others—people who used their failures and tragedies and disappointments as stepping stones for more tremendous lives. Many of my best friends are people I've never met: Oswald Chambers, George Mueller, Charles Spurgeon, A.W. Tozer, Abraham Lincoln, Jean Gietzen, and hundreds of others.

But with the Bible, don't just read it—*study* it! Digest it. Memorize it. Realize that God's greatest gift for your time on Earth is His Word.

Happy Reading!

A FATHER'S LOVE

MICHAEL T. POWERS

I have come that they may have life, and
that they may have it more abundantly.

JOHN 10:10 NKJV

His name was Brian, and he was a student at the small high school I attended. Brian was a special-education student who was constantly searching for love and attention, but it usually came for the wrong reasons. Students who wanted to have some "fun" would ask, "Brian, are you the Incredible Hulk?" He would then run down the halls roaring and flexing. He was the joke of the school and constant "entertainment" for those who watched. Brian, who was only looking for acceptance, didn't realize that they were laughing *at* him and not *with* him. One day I couldn't take it anymore. I told the other students that I had had enough of their game and to knock it off. "Aw, come on, Mike! We're just having fun. Who do you think you are anyway?"

"WHAT A FATHER SAYS TO HIS CHILDREN IS NOT HEARD BY THE WORLD; BUT IT WILL BE HEARD BY POSTERITY."

Jean Paul Richter

The teasing didn't stop for long, but Brian latched on to me that day. I stuck up for him, and now he was my buddy for life. The thought, *What will people think of me if I am friends with Brian?* swirled in my head, but I forced it out as I realized that God wanted me to treat this young man as I would want to be treated.

Later that week I invited Brian over to my house to play video games. As we sat there playing and drinking juice, he began to ask me questions like, "Hey, Mike. Where do you go to church?" I would politely answer and then turn my concentration back to the video game. But he kept on—asking me questions about God and why I was different from the other kids at school. Finally my future wife, Kristi, my high-school sweetheart at the time, pulled me aside and said, "Michael, he needs to talk. You should take him to your bedroom where you can talk privately." My wonderfully perceptive girlfriend had picked up on the cues.

When we were in my room, Brian asked again, "Hey, Mike. How come you're not like the other kids at school?" I knew then I needed to share with him the difference that God had made in my life. I got out my Bible and read John 3:16 and some verses in Romans to him. I explained that God loved him just the way he was and that He had sent Jesus down to Earth to die on a cross, rise from the dead, and make it possible for everyone, including Brian, to spend an eternity in Heaven if they believed in Him. I didn't know if Brian understood what I was telling him, but when I finished explaining, I asked him if he wanted to pray with me, and he said yes.

We prayed together: *God, I know I am a sinner, but that even if I were the only person on Earth, You still would have sent Your Son to die on the cross for me. I accept the free gift of salvation that You offer, and I ask that You now come into my heart and take control. Thank You, Lord. Amen.*

I looked at him and said, "Brian, if you meant those words you just prayed, where is Jesus right now?"

He pointed to his heart and said, "He's in here now."

Then he did something I will never forget as long as I live. Brian hugged the Bible to his chest, lay down on the bed, and let the tears flow down the sides of his cheeks. When I cry, my sobbing is usually very loud, but Brian's was strangely silent as the emotions he'd held inside let loose. When he quieted down, he said to me, "Mike, do you know that the love that God has for me must be like the love a father has for his son?"

I was floored.

Here was someone who had trouble comprehending the most simple things in school, but had now understood one of eternity's great truths. I knew now that he understood what I had shared with him.

He lay there for another five minutes or so as the salty drops continued to flow. I still remember the incredible feeling I had at that moment: it was a high, higher than anything a substance could ever give—the high of knowing that God still works miracles in everyday life. John 10:10 NIV immediately came to mind: "I have come that they may have life, and have it to the full."

It was about a week later that everything came into perspective as Brian really opened up to me. He explained that his dad had left him and his mom when he was just five years old. As Brian stood on the porch that day so many years ago, his dad had told him he was leaving because he couldn't deal with having a son like Brian anymore. Then he turned and walked out of Brian's life, never to be seen again. Brian told me that he had been looking for his dad ever since. Now I knew why the tears had flowed that day in my bedroom. His search was finally over. He found what he had been looking for since he was five years old—a father's love.

THE CHRISTMAS I GREW UP

TERRENCE CONKLIN

Honor your father and mother, that you may have a long, good life in the land the Lord your God will give you.

EXODUS 20:12 TLB

It was 4 A.M. on Christmas Eve. My father was lying in my parents' bedroom with his cardiothoracic leggings on, his heart pillow to his chest for when he coughed, and wrapped in four or five blankets to keep himself warm. He was recovering after surgery from his recent heart attack.

My little brother was sleeping on the couch and waiting for Santa to come. He hoped to "catch him in the act" this year. This was hardly unusual for this particular night of the year, if you overlooked the fact that downstairs, two other creatures were stirring—my mother and me.

With my father laid up after his brush with death, my mother was left to handle Christmas all by herself.

Everything seemed completely wrong and unfair. I watched my mother wrapping last-minute gifts, placing on the tags, and carrying them up the stairs in complete exhaustion—of course, tiptoeing past my sleeping brother.

This had not exactly been what I had in mind for my Christmas break. I was the usual selfish teenager, who had spent the last week doing nothing but trying to get out of holiday chores. After all, I was supposed to be on vacation!

As if all of that weren't bad enough, that night I was dragged to the holiday service at church. But as I watched my mother, from my position in the youth-group choir loft, something changed. I saw her in our familiar pew, sitting there without my father. She was struggling to keep my brother from wiggling. She closed her eyes in a deep prayer, and tears began to flow down her cheeks. And in that moment, as if for the first time ever, I heard the words in my heart from a familiar commandment: *Honor your father and your mother so that you may live long in the land the Lord, your God, is giving you.*

That night my mother and I stayed up into the wee hours of the morning—stuffing stockings, filling the empty space under the tree, and trying not to wake my sleeping brother by triggering the train set that now encircled the tree stand.

Seeing how much my mother had put into Christmas with an out-of-work, desperately ill husband and two young children, made me begin to respect her. I rushed to do anything she asked and did not grumble in my cranky, "teenage" way.

I wanted to honor both of my parents, always, and I would try to teach my brother to do the same—especially when "Mrs. Claus" needed help.

The Christmas lights were shining brightly upon my mother's face as we placed the last gift under the tree. But that Christmas I received a greater gift: I had learned honor and obedience and had a new hope that we would all live long in the Lord.

LIFE ISN'T FAIR!

JENNIFER H., AGE 19

(as told to T. Suzanne Eller)

There is a friend who sticks closer than a brother.

PROVERBS 18:24 NIV

I could have been described as a pretty normal teenager. I was busy with school and was an active member of my high school's junior ROTC program. My extra time was spent either working at the Subway restaurant or hanging out with friends. I loved running, juggling, playing guitar, going to the beach, surfing, partying, and basically anything fun. Although I was raised in a Christian family and went to church almost every Sunday, I didn't believe God was real. I couldn't understand how there could be so many different religions and only one true God. I was searching for some rational way to explain things.

Religion just seemed like a nice way to keep society in order. Besides, I was having fun living my life the way I was. Why should I change for some God that might not even be real?

The summer after I graduated from high school was one of the happiest times of my life. I had just turned eighteen. I was enjoying my last easygoing, fun-filled summer days before starting college at UCF. Everything was falling into place. Nothing but promise lay ahead.

All those plans took a drastic turn one hot Fourth of July afternoon. Several of my friends from work and I decided to go to a party to celebrate the holiday. There was supposed to be water skiing and volleyball, but when I arrived, everyone was just sitting around talking. Bored and hot from sitting outside, I decided to take a quick dive into the lake. I changed into my bathing suit and headed toward the dock.

I had no idea that within moments my life would never be the same.

I remember everything about the dive. I thought it was great. I had great form. Those carefree thoughts were quickly interrupted by a sudden jolt into the bottom of the shallow lake. I remember how unexpectedly my hands touched the slimy bottom. They immediately buckled, and then my head made contact. I heard a jarring sound as my neck snapped. I flipped over and lay facedown in the water.

I knew I had to get out quickly. I tried to swim, but didn't seem to be going anywhere. I opened my eyes and saw all my limbs floating motionlessly in the water. I couldn't move at all!

Extreme panic set in. Now all my concentration was focused on holding my breath. Since I've always been such a prankster, I knew my friends would think I was kidding. The longer I held my breath, the more I felt like I was going to die. I couldn't believe my life was going to end like this! I held my breath until I couldn't hold it anymore. I remember thinking, *Well, I guess this is it.* The water had started to seep into my mouth, when finally someone's hands pulled me up and out of the water.

The man who pulled me out of the water was named Kyle Mason. He had made plans to celebrate the Fourth of July with his friends. They came to pick him up, and he was walking to the parking lot when he had a sudden urge to stay home. His friends were upset at his sudden change of plans, but something told him not to go. After his friends left, Kyle noticed a party going on outside at a nearby apartment. As he was making his way over, he noticed my body floating in the lake and rushed to help.

I believe that God put him there at that moment to grab me before I started breathing water. I've never been so relieved as the moment I gulped in my first breath of air. Kyle laid me down by the waterside and questioned me, then ran to call an ambulance.

When the paramedics arrived, they called Life Flight. I watched as people stood around me. It was surreal. I couldn't move or feel anything below my shoulders. I tried to imagine spending my whole life paralyzed. Just the thought of it made me want to die right then and there.

After arriving at the hospital, my parents prayed with me as the surgery room was prepared. Their loving words and prayers were the last thing I remembered for quite some time. I spent nine days in critical condition. My lung collapsed. I developed pneumonia. A staph infection raged through my body. My parents clung to hope, but every day they were told that I probably wouldn't make it.

I was transferred to Atlanta's Shepherd Center, and things began to look a little brighter. One morning I finally woke up in the ICU. A ventilator tube spiraled out of my throat. I couldn't talk. There was something stuck down my nose, and, of course, I couldn't move. I was still pretty drugged at that point, and it all just seemed like a strange dream.

But as the weeks went on and the drugs wore off, it became more difficult to deal with the new circumstances of my life. My life had become a horrible dream that I kept expecting to wake up from.

The first month was the most difficult. It seemed like I had everything taken away from me. It was worse than the most extreme punishment, and yet it was permanent. I lost my job, car, old room, all of my favorite things—like my surfboard, guitar, juggling balls, and my bicycle—not to mention every shred of my independence.

All my dreams for my adult life had been shattered. All my rights as a human being seemed to be taken away. I remember thinking, *Why did I try so hard in life just for this to happen to me? Why did I exercise so much just to never move again?*

I started to play a game of "what ifs": *What if I had done a cannonball? What if I had just left the party?* The questions were endless and futile.

I wondered what I had done to deserve such suffering. I searched for anything possible that might have angered God. I thought maybe He was trying to get my attention. I promised God I would be as perfect as humanly possible if He would just give me another chance. This phase lasted only days, and then I slipped back into my doubts, disbelief, and questions.

At first I thought I would regain movement. Walking wasn't my greatest concern, but I hoped to move my arms. I could not wait for the day when I would be able to take care of all my own personal needs, play my guitar, or just give someone a hug.

Finally I had no choice but to accept the possibility that I might never move anything again. It was depressing to say good-bye to everything I had ever known. I stared at my old pictures all day, and I cried.

In the middle of physical therapy one morning, the song "Happy" by Sister Hazel filled the room. Immediately the memories flooded my mind. Everything had been perfect then. I was at a Fourth of July celebration watching fireworks, listening to Sister Hazel play, hanging out with all my friends, and having a great time living a normal life.

I wanted to be that girl again. She could laugh. She knew how to have fun. She was happy. She didn't belong in a wheelchair. As the song played, I cried. I wanted my old life back, but as much as I did not want to believe that this had happened, there was no way around it. I had to deal with it sooner or later.

I distinctly remember the day I started to accept my injury. It was the second month after the accident, and I was crying, thinking about what my life had become. Only this time I felt something different. It finally clicked. There was no changing what had happened, so I had to pick up the pieces that I could and move on. I had to stop feeling sorry for myself and try to press forward the best I could. That was the good news, but the bad news was that I stopped crying out to God. I decided to prove to my friends that I was the same person I had been before the accident.

Then September 11, 2001, happened. The attacks made me realize how fragile and uncertain our lives are. I wanted to give

God a chance. As I sorted through these thoughts, I stumbled across a Web site of a man who had also broken his neck in a diving accident. He shared the peace and indescribable beauty of his short glimpse into Heaven when he faced his near-death experience. As I read his story, I realized that I had found my answer. This man's story made me face my own memories. I suddenly remembered that immediately after I was pulled out of the water, I frantically told everyone that I was lost. The moment I was faced with death, I knew I had not lived my life for God. The thought of eternity was not peaceful at all.

When I was in critical condition, I had no visions of peace, but rather complete darkness. I was terrified, and all I wanted was to find a way out of my situation.

I knew that it was time to open my heart to God.

I constantly sought God from that point on, and He never failed me when I did. As soon as I understood how real and powerful He is, it was frightening to think about all the sin that was once a part of my life. As I faced God, I shook and cried, but God got a hold of me in such a strong way. There's no other way to explain it. God opened my eyes, and all I could do was crumble before Him.

I'm so glad God has given me a new life, one where I look forward to each new day with God as my best friend.

THE "IN" CROWD

IAN WHITFIELD

Better is one day in your courts than a thousand elsewhere.

PSALM 84:10 NIV

Have you ever wished you were someone else? I have!

I was raised in a great family with seven brothers and sisters. My parents were missionaries in Africa for many years, so I naturally had a lot of knowledge about God and Christianity. At a young age, I decided to begin a relationship with God through Jesus Christ.

As I grew older, I became increasingly involved in sports and friends, and my faith became a less important part of my life. Instead, I focused on myself and on ensuring that, wherever I was, I was always part of the "in" group. People often thought I had it "all together." However, on the inside, I was very unsure of myself. In high school I spent a lot of time working out in the gym. I thought that if I looked good, then I would feel better inside. The problem was this: there was always someone bigger

"THERE IS A GOD-SHAPED VACUUM IN EVERY MAN, WOMAN, AND CHILD THAT CANNOT BE FILLED BY ANY MAN-MADE OBJECT— ONLY BY GOD MADE KNOWN BY HIS SON, JESUS CHRIST."

Blaise Pascal

and stronger than I was. I always wished I had the gifts and abilities of others. But instead, I was just Ian Whitfield—your average guy.

In college, I became interested again in my spiritual journey, but was afraid to give God full control of all areas of my life. I thought He would ask me to be someone I didn't want to be. In hindsight, I realize how foolish this was; but it was my reality at the time. I tried to fill the emptiness I felt with other things: sports, relationships, and school.

In my second year, a close friend of mine was killed in a car accident. I pictured myself in that situation, and I knew I was not ready to die; I still had too many unanswered questions. Around that time, another friend had been talking to me about his faith in God and his relationship with Jesus Christ. I called him immediately. He shared with me how God had not left me; rather, I had left Him. I had not nurtured my relationship with Jesus. I needed to renew the friendship with Christ that I had begun so many years before.

Shortly after that I recommitted my life to God.

Blaise Pascal, the great French mathematician, once said: "There is a God-shaped vacuum in every man, woman, and child that cannot be filled by any man-made object—only by God made known by His Son, Jesus Christ." I realized that I had spent much of my life trying to stuff all sorts of things into the void in my heart, which could only be filled by God.

Since that time, I have experienced a great deal of inner peace, even during difficult times, including the death of my father. It has not been an easy journey; but I wouldn't trade a day with God for a thousand elsewhere. I still have challenges, but now I turn immediately to God for help and hope instead of trying to do it on my own. I still admire the gifts and abilities of others, but I no longer wish to be someone else. Today I am happy with who God made me to be and with my special relationship with Him.

THE LITTLE GIRL WHO FEARED DEATH

TANYA KOZLOVA

The free gift of God is eternal life.

ROMANS 6:23 TLB

> "DEATH IS THE GOLDEN KEY THAT OPENS THE PALACE OF ETERNITY."
>
> John Milton

When I was a little girl, I used to wake up in the middle of the night with fear in my heart—the terrifying fear of death. I was in despair because I did not know what would happen to me after I died. I thought there would be nothing and that would be the end. As a little girl, I would run to my parents' room in tears, asking, "Mama, am I going to die?" Despite my otherwise happy childhood, this nightmare haunted my heart.

While growing up, I learned to drive this fear deep inside myself. Yet, I was always wondering what would happen after I died. Death scared me, but life went on. Sports and money became most important to me, because they gave me self-confidence, independence, and pride in myself. I alone decided what was good and what was bad. Everything I had been taught by my parents became of minor importance. I had no interest in the lives of people around me. Yet, despite the importance and success I had achieved, I still had no answer to the question of what would happen to me when I died. I had outward strength and beauty, but fear was killing me on the inside. *Why live,* I wondered, *if I have to die all the same?* Only God, the One who had created me, could answer this question.

I heard about God for the first time from my best girlfriend. At first, it seemed more like a fairy tale. Yet, I was fascinated with the possibility of receiving eternal life. My friend shared that all it took was simply believing in Jesus Christ. It seemed that I was getting closer and closer, and finally I found an answer to the question that had troubled me all my life. God giving us eternal life was a discovery. As an eighteen-year-old, I went running to my mother in tears, just as I had done in my childhood. Only my words were different this time: "Mama, I'm not afraid of death anymore. Christ has given me eternal life!"

Since then, four years have passed. My greatest joy is that all my family—my parents and sisters—now believe in Christ. God showed me a wonderful way, and I chose it. This year, I graduated from Bible college in Moscow. I want to tell the people of my country about our great, loving God, who gives love, joy, happiness, and, above all else, meaning to life.

BETWEEN MY TWO WORLDS

CARRIE R., AGE 16

(as told to T. Suzanne Eller)

Believe on the Lord Jesus Christ, and you will be saved.

ACTS 16:31 NKJV

I used to be what is commonly referred to as a "church brat." In fact, I was in church from the time I was born. I grew up believing that if I acted a certain way and attended church, then I was all right. Church was a weekly habit for me. I heard from others about the joy of a changed life, but somehow I never experienced that feeling.

When I was thirteen, I started having trouble in school. I fought with my parents constantly. Then I lost two friends—one died in a car wreck, and the other walked away from our friendship.

One summer our youth group attended an awesome revival in another city. I went to the altar thinking I would find what was missing in my life, but I didn't. I began to wonder if God would ever have any use for me. Before long, the sadness I carried around with me turned to a silent bitterness.

Over the next two years, I developed quite an attitude. I missed church whenever I had the opportunity. I hated nearly every moment of the youth service when I had to go, but I put on a fake smile and a pretense that all was okay. The truth is, I was lying through my teeth. Alone, I would sit and curse myself. I started wearing a lot of dark clothing, and I listened to music that echoed my thoughts.

I didn't like other people at all, and I seized any moment to surround myself with silence. I started reading books about witchcraft. A friend of mine claimed to be a witch, and I asked her to show me how to cast spells. Ironically, the entire time I was involved in witchcraft, I was also showing up for church activities and Teens-4-Christ at school. I seemed to be in a constant blur, torn between two worlds.

In the summer of 2000, I pleaded with God, saying, *Please come back into my life. I'll try harder!* I tried to be different. I attended church more. I prayed a little more. I quit wearing black clothing and attempted to leave my dark thoughts behind. But whatever I was doing didn't seem to work. I failed again, because I thought I could do it all by myself.

Then came my next battle: hormones! I had never really had a thing for guys before, but when I turned fifteen, the sight of an attractive guy made my heart pump into overtime.

I was extremely attracted to this one guy. We ended up going out, but not in the best way. What was weird was that while he wanted to grow in God, I was satisfied with being lukewarm.

One day he ended the relationship, telling me that God had led him to do it. I was deeply hurt and angry, but there was nothing I could do. One month later he called. He wanted to try to get together again, but this time with Christ as part of our relationship. He had caught me in the worst time imaginable. I didn't care about life. I didn't care for anyone. I didn't trust anyone. And yet, we renewed our relationship based on his hopes and my apathy.

Less than two months later, the same old temptations plagued us, and he broke up with me for the last time. He said that God couldn't honor our relationship as it was. Crying and protesting, I let him go.

One of my friends at school, Tiffany, introduced me to a girl named Stephanie. Stephanie was a grade ahead of me, and we were in band together. On the first day of early band, Stephanie and I sat together. I noticed something different about her, but I couldn't really put my finger on it. As the year progressed,

Tiffany, Stephanie, and I became close. Stephanie asked me to join her and Tiffany at church.

After several invitations, I finally accepted and went with her to church on a Wednesday night. The pastor wasn't like any youth pastor I'd ever seen, with his casual attire, spiky blond hair, and goatee. I was somewhat confused when church began and was puzzled all through the service. This was not the usual youth church meeting. People worshiped God as if they *knew* Him. The whole time my mind was thinking, *What are they doing? Why did they say that? Huh, I've never felt this before.*

When the youth pastor asked people to come to the altar, even though my self-righteous pride told me earlier not to make any moves and not to wimp out, I snapped. I knelt at the altar, and tears poured down my face. I trembled as I experienced God. I felt a wave of peace wash over me.

At 8:46 P.M. on that Wednesday night, I rededicated my heart to the Lord. This time it meant something, and it wasn't done out of guilt.

Sure, I made mistakes more than once after that night. I got involved with this guy. I knew he wasn't where he needed to be with God, but something in me said it was okay. I should've ignored that little something. I ended that relationship in less than a month, and it was a relief.

I made a commitment to God after that mistake. I was tired of taking chances and making mistakes, so I made a promise not to go after any more guys for a while. I decided to wait until God sent the one He had chosen for me.

I've now pierced my right ear, and I continue to wear only one earring as a symbol and reminder of this promise. When God sends His chosen partner for my life, then I'll either take out the earring or get my left ear pierced. So if you see me now, look for that one earring. It is my oath to God.

Things are different now and I'm growing so much. Through the help of the Holy Spirit, I'm learning to trust God and others. I'm healing. I've given up my old bad habits. My mind is refreshed and clean. I listen to music that lifts up Christ. At last, I feel His love, and I'm not afraid to praise Him. I'm not a "church brat" anymore.

I'm a believer.

THE BIBLE THAT JUST WOULDN'T GO AWAY

LENA MABRA

**The whole Bible was given to us by inspiration
from God and is useful to teach us what is true
and to make us realize what is wrong in our lives;
it straightens us out and helps us do what is right.**

2 TIMOTHY 3:16 TLB

Have you ever had something in life that just wouldn't go away? Some of you may recall a stray dog or cat that showed up and made itself at home. Others may say that your bills or taxes never go away. Maybe a guest who is no longer a guest but a tax write-off might be what comes to your mind. Well, mine was a Bible.

Yes, it was the Bible that just wouldn't go away. At the end of my first week at a Christian university, a friend discovered that I didn't have a Bible and gave me an old one that she had. The cover was barely hanging on as five pieces of thread held on for dear life. I used an old pillow sham to give the book a new cover. Although I didn't really care for the fabric, it made do.

The Bible served me for two years as I referred to it many times for classes and personal devotions. There were hundreds of markings as I made notes in the margins after reading a Scripture. There were even yellowed tearstains splattered on the silly fabric cover from the many times I spent alone with that Bible and God.

However, as I became a "much better Christian," I decided that I needed a Bible that would match my "spiritual maturity." I bought a beautiful leather-bound version with my name embossed in gold. Oh, I was so proud to carry it around with me. I even purchased an expensive cover for it like all the other Christians seemed to have. Never mind that I hardly took the time to read it anymore—it gave the impression that I wanted others to see, a sort of status symbol.

Then, cleaning up my dorm room one day, I discovered the dusty old Bible under my bed. Since I thought it was a shame to throw away God's Word, I decided to leave it down the hall by someone else's door. A few weeks later, it returned at my doorstep with a note that read, "Sorry you left your Bible. Thought you'd really need it, so I'm glad to return it to you." No signature was given.

I took the embarrassing Bible with its pathetic pillowcase cover across campus and left it in the business department. Saying a small mental good-bye, I figured it was gone for good. That very week, it appeared again at my door. The card stated, "You must have left this while studying. I'm sure you really need it." Again, no signature.

By now, I was starting to get a little annoyed. *Why can't someone just leave the thing where I put it, or at least pick it up and make it their own? Why can't I just pitch it in the dumpster? Ugggghh!"* I was getting frustrated.

I threw the flowered fabric-covered book in my duffle bag and took it with me to a friend's house in another state. Leaving the Bible out in a field of nowhere felt wrong, but it was, on the other hand, a bit of a relief that I could finally end this silly game.

Five months later, I received a package wrapped in plain brown paper with no return address. It was my Bible! The letter said, "Since you left your Bible and the contact information was written in the front, I am happy to return this to you. I'm sure you've been needing it."

Out of all the versions I own, my children love this one the best. And my youngest tells me with all the enthusiasm of a five-year-old angel, "Mommy, I just love this pretty, pretty cover because it makes me happy!"

Needless to say, I knew that it was meant for me to hold on to this Bible. It has been in my life for eighteen years now, and I've referred to it many times, amazed to find the journaling of my development as a Christian and an individual.

Everyday I'm thankful for the Bible that wouldn't go away—Someone knew I really needed it!

IF YOU ARE REAL...

T. SUZANNE ELLER

Behold, what manner of love the Father hath bestowed upon us, that we should be called the sons of God.

1 JOHN 3:1

The small church was crowded. All around me people worshiped a God that I didn't believe existed. Why was I there? My neighbors had asked me to come, and to be honest, I was hoping they'd leave me alone after that if I did.

I wasn't sure what to expect. I had attended services with my family a few times, but it was more of a ritual or a way to celebrate holidays. What I hadn't anticipated was the wetness pressed against my eyelids as I clenched them shut.

My motto? Never let them see you cry. I wasn't about to break down in front of people I didn't even know. I wasn't crying because I felt the presence of God or because I sensed His love for me. I was fighting tears of anger—I was so mad that I shook inside. How dare the preacher stand there and talk about the love of God?! It was easy for him and people like him to spout off about a God who existed, who had a purpose for every person. Well, maybe their God had taken a personal interest in them, but He certainly didn't live at my house.

The mother I am about to share with you is not the same mom I have now. You see, she had an encounter with God, and He brought her out of the darkness of emotional pain and healed her. But in order to share my story, I have to share a little bit of hers as well.

My mom left home at sixteen years old, pregnant and newly married to a boy who thought he was a man. She lost her first baby to cystic fibrosis when the toddler was less than two years old. She had her second child at age eighteen, and she was abandoned by her husband at the age of twenty-one. Later he came to visit her one night and forced her to have sex. She discovered two weeks later she was pregnant.

I was that baby.

Mom later married a good man who loved both her and her two little kids who came as a package deal. But in spite of this turn of events, my mom was fragile. Like stained glass, she was pretty on the outside, but the broken pieces of her life created the portrait.

Growing up, I never knew what to expect. Would it be the mom who brought home suckers to surprise us or the woman who spouted, ran out the door, and threatened to kill herself? These episodes were always followed with tearful requests for forgiveness.

Don't get me wrong, it wasn't always bad in my home, but when it was, it was loud, chaotic, and frightening. I feared one day that my mom would pull the trigger or hurt herself. I hated the words that came out of her mouth when she was angry.

One day my mom chased me through the house, brandishing an umbrella as she screamed at me. I ran out the door and into the rain. I was wearing a T-shirt and jeans, but no shoes. The cold rain pelted me as I ran down Latimer Street. I pushed through the wetness, pumping my arms and running as fast as I could. Finally I stopped, bending down to catch my breath as my tears meshed with the raindrops. I slowly turned around, walked home, sat on the curb, and wept.

I was stuck. I couldn't run away. I had no money, no place to go. I was thirteen years old. Where would I go?

I started smoking at the bus stop, pushing boundaries with my teachers, and drinking with my best friend. My attempts to be tough must have appeared hilarious to others. I was skinny to a fault and looked younger than my age. Being tough didn't come natural. My heart was gentle, and I hated conflict and fighting, yet every single time I let my guard down, it seemed that someone would wound my already fragile spirit.

That's when the hardness crept in. *Never let them see you cry. Never give them a chance to know you care.*

One day my mom pulled us into her bedroom. She put a gun to her head and threatened to shoot herself. I was scared, not because I thought she would die, but because under my breath I found myself whispering, "Just do it."

Who is this person I was becoming? I wondered.

My mom did not pull the trigger. I don't think she ever intended to, but instead was crying out for help. As a child, I had no way of recognizing that, though today I do.

Two years later I stood in the little church. The pastor sang, strumming on the guitar as people knelt at the altar. "He loves you," he said. "He has a plan for your life."

Yeah, right, I thought. I pointed my chin at the sky, eyes closed, and I challenged this God of whom he spoke. "If You are real," I whispered, "and I don't believe You are, but if You exist and You know me and You love me like he says, I need to know."

I expected nothing, yet I received everything as a tender touch reached through my hardened heart. I've had trouble explaining this moment to people over the years. "Did you see God?" No. "Did you feel God's presence?" Yes, but it was subtle and deep inside of me, touching areas that I had closed long ago to everyone, and I knew it was God.

Tears broke, streaming down my cheeks, and for the first time in a long time, I wept. I felt as if God had wrapped me in a warm blanket, enclosing me in His love. I stumbled from the church. I ran home and tried to tell my mom what had just happened to me, though I didn't fully understand what had occurred.

Did everything magically change? No. My circumstances were still the same, but everything was different on the inside of me.

I made mistakes, huge blunders, as I tried to learn what it meant to follow Jesus and acknowledge Him as my Savior. I wasn't perfect, but I understood His love and I knew that I wanted to know more. There were times when I wept at the altar and then went home to chaos. There were times when I fell in my walk with Christ, but the gentle encouragement of my new church family helped me to keep going.

It is amazing what can happen when God restores a broken life. It can be beautiful like the portrait that my mom is now, the shattered pieces of her life assembled together in a lovely picture of God's mercy.

Today I am a mother myself. I am also an author, a public speaker, and a wife. I have had the opportunity to minister to teens and women across the nation, sharing the story of my life, the beauty of purpose, and the transforming power of God's tremendous love. My mother and father gave their lives to God when I was in my junior year of high school. I found a note from my dad under my pillow one day. I still carry it with me, the tattered pieces are a reminder of what God has done. My quiet father, who very rarely shared the depth of his emotions, said in that letter, "I have watched you, and I see that you have something that is of great worth, a treasure. I know that it is real, and I admire you for your faith and your love for God."

We have never spoken of that letter, but it came at a time when I had prayed for a sign, saying, *God, show me that You hear my prayers. Heal my family. Let me know that You are listening.* The folded piece of paper under my pillow was Heaven-sent and priceless.

For years now, my mom and I have been the best of friends. She is compassionate, loving, and whole, and the memories of our past are forgiven and long forgotten.

Today I am still running after the same God who touched my life when I was fifteen. I always tell my teen audiences that one day I'll be an old woman running after God with my walker. You see, He's done a million things for me. He's been with me through difficult times, but my love for Him will always be wrapped around that first moment when He reached down to an angry, hurting, skinny, fifteen-year-old and silently whispered that He loved me.

And I still find myself whispering back, "I love You too."

SPRAY PAINTING FOR JESUS

BEN BRYDEN

(as told to Barbara Major Bryden)

"You will go wherever I send you and speak whatever I tell you to. And don't be afraid of the people, for I, the Lord, will be with you and see you through." Then he touched my mouth and said, "See, I have put my words in your mouth!"

JEREMIAH 1:7-9 TLB

Armed with stencils and bright colors of spray paint, we stepped out of the air-conditioned bus. Justin and I hurried toward the first condo on the short street. The other high-school teams spread out to cover the rest of the buildings.

"Hey, Ben. If you talk to this family, I'll talk to the people at the next house," said Justin breathlessly.

"Sounds good," I answered.

Dodging a large hanging plant, I rang the doorbell. A man with a little girl in his arms opened the door. "We're painting house numbers on curbs," I said. "Could we do yours? If you have your house number on the curb, it's easier for emergency vehicles to find your home. And it's free."

The man gave me a puzzled look and asked with a Spanish accent, "What do you want?"

I realized the man hadn't understood.

Wow! I finally get to use my Spanish. Hope I know enough words to explain. I switched to Spanish, searched for the right words, and explained again slowly.

The man next door came over when he heard us talking and started listening as well.

"Sure. Go ahead. What group are you with?" asked the little girl's father in a mix between Spanish and English.

"We're attending the Christian youth conference at the university."

"Oh," said the man settling into a chair on the porch with his daughter on his lap. "My wife is cooking for your group. That's why I'm taking care of our daughter."

We painted the numbers on the curb as the two men watched from the shade.

"Good thing you can speak Spanish, Ben," Justin whispered to me as we worked. When we finished painting, I peeled the tape back, Justin pulled the stencils off, and we walked back to the porch where the little group was sitting.

"Thanks. Do you mind if I ask you some questions? We're supposed to fill out this survey form."

"What do you want to know?"

I read each question slowly, translating the English into Spanish. Both men began to discuss the questions: How do you like living so close to the university? Are the young people at the conference too noisy? Do you believe in the God of the Bible? Do you attend church? Do you have any questions you would like to ask?

"I always wanted to hear about Jesus, but there was no one to ask," interrupted the next-door neighbor moving closer.

I looked at him and saw real hunger in his eyes. *Lord, he wants me to tell him about You! I'm not sure I have enough Spanish to tell him what he needs to know. Somehow, Lord, give me the right words.*

First, I told him everything I could think of about Jesus. I was still worried my high-school Spanish didn't include all the words I needed to share about Jesus, but the words came anyhow. I was using words I couldn't even remember learning in Spanish class, but the men understood and so did I. Finally, I asked the neighbor if we could pray with him to accept Christ into his life.

"Yes. You're the first one to explain it to me, so I can understand."

"Repeat this prayer after me," I instructed him. I was shaking all over, I was so excited, when I began the sinner's prayer in Spanish.

"I know Jesus loves me! I know it!" the neighbor exclaimed, shaking our hands after the prayer. "What do I do now?" His eyes were dancing, and he looked like he could hear angels singing.

We pulled out our list of area churches. We were so excited it was hard to concentrate. Finally, we found a church close to his home. Then we prayed with him again.

As Justin and I started back to the bus, my thoughts were whirling. *I can't believe that happened to me! I didn't know those words.*

Oh, Lord, I prayed excitedly, *that was the most amazing thing that has ever happened to me! You gave me words I didn't have and didn't even know, and You gave me their translation, so I could tell that man about You. I trusted You, and You gave me what I needed. Now I want to tell more people about You! Thank You, Lord.*

A CHRISTMAS DELIVERY

STEFANIE MORRIS

"The meek and lowly are fortunate!
For the whole wide world belongs to them."

MATTHEW 5:5 TLB

As soon as I turned south, the houses became smaller, the paint more chipped and faded. I began to feel a little nervous. *I should have waited until someone could deliver these Christmas gifts with me,* I thought.

I knew this neighborhood had a high crime rate. 9200…9426…9614…I was getting a little closer. I felt anxious, hoping that I had the right address. Each year, our youth group raised money to buy Christmas gifts for boys and girls whose parents were in prison. This year we were given the names of two twin boys. Their grandparents were raising them while their mom served time. As far as I knew, there was no dad.

9806....This was it. I pulled up in front of a small house. There was no one in sight and no car in the driveway. *God, I prayed, I am delivering these gifts for You. I need You to protect me!*

I carefully locked the car door before walking up to the house. To my surprise, a tall young man answered the door. I didn't hear any sounds of either children or grandparents.

"Hello, I'm looking for Jackie Brown..." I paused, but the young man didn't say a word.

"I have some Christmas gifts that his daughter, Tanya, asked me to buy for her children," I explained.

"Uh, sure," the young man replied and said nothing more. I still had no way of knowing if I was at the right house. Then he cracked open the door and shouted: "Matthew, get out here." A second young man walked out. There was still no sign of the children or their grandparents.

God, I'm trusting You, I prayed silently.

I knew many people, including my grandmother, would think I was behaving foolishly. But I was showing the love of Christ to the needy for Christmas, and I was going to trust Him for my protection. As an act of faith, I deliberately turned my back on the young men and led them to the trunk of my car.

The cynical part of me whispered that there might not be a Jackie Brown at this house and that these young men might be leading me on just to get free Christmas gifts. Still, I began to hand the gifts over to them.

As I handed Matthew the last present, a football, I said a prayer in my heart: *Lord, let these gifts be the right ones that will bring joy to their Christmas.*

Proud of my feeble faith, I refused to think one nervous thought as I followed the men into the dark and silent house. Almost immediately I saw an elderly gentlemen seated in a faded chair. *Thank You, Jesus!* I prayed silently.

"Mr. Jackie Brown?" I asked. He nodded. His face was lean and lined, a visible reminder to the passage of many years. "I'm Stefanie Morris.

"Tanya asked us to buy gifts for her children," I explained. "She also wanted us to tell them that she loves them very much." As I delivered Tanya's message, I looked over at the eight-year-old twins.

They were playing near a Christmas tree and looked happy and healthy. But there were no presents under the tree, and the house was sparsely furnished. It felt good to help a family that was clearly in need.

"Praise the Lord! He always provides," Jackie Brown said, looking at the gifts the young men carried. I took a seat while they placed the gifts under the tree. The twins immediately began poking, prodding, and weighing the wrapped gifts excitedly. Suddenly one boy gave a joyful shout, "It's a football!"

Yes, the Lord always provides, I agreed silently.

"I grew up in the Depression," Mr. Brown explained. "Life was hard. There were ten of us. We were poor, but we didn't know it. We were in the country, so we farmed and hunted. We never had much, but we always had enough. The good Lord may appear to be slow, but He is never late."

I was moved. Life had been hard for Jackie Brown. He was probably in his late 60s or early 70s. He was not in the physical or financial position to take care of these children, but they needed him, so he relied on God.

Jackie repeated the phrase that seemed to be the motto of his life: "Yes, the good Lord is never late." Then he asked me the very question I had been hoping to ask him, "Do you know the Lord?"

I felt humbled and close to tears. I had come to this house determined to show the love of Christ. Instead, I found a little home already full of His self-sacrificial love. I had been proud of my fragile, trembling faith that took me through their door. Inside, I found a frail man with a stronger faith than I had ever known. He had learned to trust God for his daily bread through decades of hardship.

I came to bring Christmas joy. Yet, Christmas was already there. The baby Jesus was born to just such a home as this.

"Praise God," I replied. "Yes, Jackie, I have seen the Lord!"

A PROMISE KEPT

KRISTI POWERS

**If a man vow a vow unto the LORD…he shall not break his word,
he shall do according to all that proceedeth out of his mouth.**

NUMBERS 30:2

My father was not a sentimental man. I don't remember him ever "ooohhing" or "ahhing" over something I made as a child. Don't get me wrong—I knew that my dad loved me, but getting all mushy-eyed was not his thing. I learned that he showed me love in other ways.

There was one particular time in my life when this became truly real to me. I had always believed that my parents had a good marriage, but just before I, the youngest of four children, turned sixteen, my belief was sorely tested. My father, who used to share in the chores around the house, gradually started becoming despondent. From the time he came home from his job at the factory until the time he went to bed, he hardly spoke a word to my mom or us kids. The strain on my mom and dad's relationship was very evident. However, I was not prepared for the day that Mom sat my siblings and me down and told us that Dad had decided to leave our home. All I could think was that I was going to be a product of a divorced family. It was something I had never thought possible, and it grieved me greatly. I kept telling myself that it wasn't really going to happen, but I went totally numb when I realized that my dad was actually leaving.

The night before he left, I stayed in my room for a long time. I prayed and I cried—and I wrote a long letter to my dad. I told him how much I loved him and how much I would miss him. I told him that I was praying for him and wanted him to know that no matter what, Jesus and I loved him. I told him that I would always and forever be his Krissie...his "Noodles." As I folded my note, I stuck in a picture of me with a saying I had always heard: "Anyone can be a father, but it takes someone special to be a daddy."

Early the next morning, as my dad was getting ready to leave our house, I snuck out to the car and slipped my letter into one of his bags.

Two weeks went by with hardly a word from my father. Then one afternoon, I came home from school to find my mom sitting at the dining-room table, waiting to talk to me. I could see in her eyes that she had been crying. She told me that Dad had been there and that they had talked for a long time. They'd decided that there were things that they could work on, changes they could make—and that their marriage was worth saving. Mom then turned her focus to my eyes—"Kristi, Dad told me that you wrote him a letter. Can I ask what you wrote to him?"

I found it hard to share with my mom what I had written from my heart to my dad. I mumbled a few words and shrugged. And then Mom told me, "Dad said that when he read your letter, it made him cry. It meant a lot to him, and I have hardly ever seen your dad cry. After he read your letter, he called to ask if he could come over to talk. Whatever you said really made a difference to your dad."

A few days later my dad was back, this time to stay. We never talked about the letter, my dad and I. But I knew there was an unspoken promise that he would always be there for me.

My parents went on to be married a total of thirty-six years before my dad's early death at the age of fifty-three, cutting short their lives together. In the last sixteen years of my parents' marriage, I, and all those who knew my mom and dad, witnessed one of the truly "great" marriages. Their love grew stronger every day, and my heart swelled with pride as I saw them grow closer together.

When Mom and Dad received the news from the doctor that his heart was rapidly deteriorating, they took it hand in hand, side by side, all the way. After Dad's death, we had the most unpleasant task of going through his things. I didn't really want to be involved in that process, so I opted to run errands while most of Dad's things were divided and boxed up.

When I got back from my errand, my brother said, "Kristi, Mom said to give this to you. She said you would know what it meant." As I looked down into his outstretched hand, it was then that I knew the impact that my letter had had that day so long ago. In my brother's hand was the picture I'd given my dad. My unsentimental dad, who never let his emotions get the best of him, my dad, who almost never outwardly showed his love for me, had kept the one thing that meant so much to him—and to me.

I sat down and the tears began to flow, tears that I thought had dried up from the grief of his death, but that had now found new life as I realized what I had meant to him. Mom told me that Dad kept both the picture and that letter his whole life.

In my home I have a box that I call the "Dad box." In it are so many things that remind me of him. I pull that picture out every once in a while and remember. I remember a promise that was made many years ago between a young man and his bride on their wedding day, and I remember the unspoken promise that was made between a father and his daughter....

A promise kept.

WHEN I WAS A PRODIGAL SON

DON HALL

(as told to Nanette Thorsen-Snipes)

"'This son of mine was dead and has now returned to life.

He was lost, but now he is found.'"

LUKE 15:24 NLT

At the age of seventeen, I found myself sitting in a jail cell, wondering how things could have gone so wrong in my life. I didn't know it then, but looking back, I felt a lot like the prodigal son of the Bible.

It was two days after Thanksgiving. Clouds were slung low across the sky and overshadowing with rain that cold day in 1983. My mom, my stepdad, Jim, and my younger brother and sister had gone to the grocery store. Before they got home, the phone rang, and I answered it.

"A MAN MAY GO TO HEAVEN WITHOUT HEALTH, WITHOUT RICHES, WITHOUT HONOR, WITHOUT LEARNING, WITHOUT FRIENDS, BUT HE CAN NEVER GO THERE WITHOUT CHRIST."

John Dyer

After asking for my mother, the person on the phone said, "Tell her that Benny hung himself." It felt as though someone struck me in the gut. Benny was my dad.

"Is he dead?" I asked, holding my breath and hoping it wasn't true. I couldn't even cry. But the pain left an empty hole in me because I didn't really know my dad. When the answer came back, "Yes," I sat down to absorb what had happened.

A flood of memories came back. It seemed like a rerun of one of those unbelievable, yet true, stories. My mother had faced my dad's rage one weekend—at the end of a gun. She finally talked him into putting it down. After he went to work, she packed our bags and we moved out. My brother was seven and I was four, yet I vividly remember being in the motel room where we hid out for a week. I had on my cowboy outfit that day, and Mom was crying.

Maybe that's one reason why I stayed angry all those years. I was angry at my father for trying to hurt Mom. Later, I was angry because he died before I could get to know him.

Nothing ever went right for me after my dad died. I couldn't concentrate or learn. I finally quit school in the tenth grade. I went to work as a roofer, a carpet cleaner, anything I could do to earn money.

My anger continued to grow. I often made life miserable for everyone by drinking. Alcohol brought on more anger, which made me lose my temper. It was nothing for me to put my fist through a wall or kick in a door. I was arrested several times for driving under the influence of alcohol.

One day, I became angry because the bike I'd bought wasn't working right. I picked the ten-speed bicycle up over my head and began screaming obscenities. I slammed it repeatedly into the ground until it lay in a crumpled heap.

Mom and Jim became alarmed at my uncontrollable rage and took me to see a counselor. I had nothing to say to a shrink. I just sat there and waited for him to quit talking. After the third session, he gave up and told Mom he couldn't help me if I wouldn't communicate, which suited me just fine.

My drinking worsened, and I had bouts with depression, staying in bed for days. I also started hanging out with bad company and earned myself some dangerous enemies.

One day a bullet hit my car as I drove down the highway. When someone kicked down the basement door, which led to my bedroom, I, too, became alarmed. I guess that's why I took the gun from my parents' closet. I never kept it loaded, but its presence made me feel safe.

The next evening I drove to the hotel where my brother worked. After parking my car, I went straight toward the bar.

Inside, a strong, burly man said, "Son, I need to see your ID." Because I didn't have one, I tried to muscle my way past the guy. He became angry and shoved me. I shoved back. The next thing I knew, he smacked me in the jaw and I hit the floor. I jumped up, waving the gun in his face.

Meanwhile someone had called the police, and in a split second I heard them say, "Freeze!" I turned to my left where three policemen stood in a firing stance, their guns drawn and aimed directly at me. To my right, I looked down the barrel of another officer's gun. The scene was chaotic. The police shouted, "Drop your weapon! Get your hands up on the wall!" I was then handcuffed and taken to jail.

So, for the fourth or fifth time, I sat in the county jail with the stench of bodily fluids and sweaty men surrounding me. I didn't worry. Whenever I was caught driving under the influence of alcohol, my parents always posted bail for me. So I was shocked when I called for them to get me out and Mom said no.

I didn't realize at the time that they had been praying for me. They had decided to let go and entrust me to God. But all I could see were the bars on that jail cell and no way out. I paced the floor like a wild animal. After a while, I knew I was in real trouble, so I said a simple prayer: *God, please help me. All I want is a decent life.*

A few days later, a friend and his father posted bail for me. Angrily, I went home and packed my things, never once speaking to my parents. Then I moved in with my friend.

Within a year, I met a beautiful young woman. We later married and now have two wonderful children. Several months after we married, my wife and I both turned our lives over to God. In fact, I began spending many of my evenings sharing my story with men in state prisons. I told them about God and his miraculous transformation of my life.

I still regret all the pain I caused my parents. One recent Christmas, while my wife and the kids were at Mom's, my stepdad and I went to the grocery store. While in the cab of the truck with music softly playing in the background, I said, "Jim, can you ever forgive me for all the pain I've put you through?"

The man I knew as my dad looked at me and smiled. "I've already forgiven you, Donnie," he said. Then he put his arm around me. I couldn't help thinking of the Prodigal Son and how our Heavenly Father always welcomes us home too.

FRIENDS TO THE END

JEANINE WOLFE

Wounds from a friend are better

than many kisses from an enemy.

PROVERBS 27:6 NLT

"Friends to the end!" Breana had signed the picture of us that hung on my bedroom wall. We were so happy the night it was taken, all confidence and smiles.

Breana's handwritten promise looped and curled with the joy we had shared. "Friends to the end," and I was the one who ended it.

We had been friends for ten years, since the day I'd moved in next door, the summer just before second grade. I was standing on the sidewalk watching the moving van being unloaded and then, there was Breana, straddling her bike beside me.

"That your bike?" She pointed at the pink bike my father was wheeling into the garage.

"LOTS OF PEOPLE WANT TO RIDE WITH YOU IN THE LIMO, BUT WHAT YOU WANT IS SOMEONE WHO WILL TAKE THE BUS WITH YOU WHEN THE LIMO BREAKS DOWN."

Oprah Winfrey

"Yes."

"Wanna ride to the park?"

"Sure."

Just that simply, we became friends. More really. We were next-door sisters.

Maybe if I could look back and say, "That is the moment our friendship ended," I could repair it. But there wasn't a dramatic split. I made one choice, one step, one rip at a time, until I had walked away from Breana and into my new life with my new friends.

I guess I could really say that Breana started it. It was her idea for me to try out for cheerleading. "You're the best dancer in our class and the best gymnast in the club. You'd be a natural."

"You're crazy," I protested, though I really did believe her and I did want to try out. I knew that Breana knew that. It was her job to talk me into it, then if I failed, it would have been all her idea and I could shrug it off with a "What did I tell you?"

I finally gave in when Breana promised to try out with me. She went to all the practices, learned the routines, and spent two weeks in the backyard coaching me.

Breana was as excited as I was when I made the squad and more surprised than I was when she did too.

The night of our first football game, Breana gave me a cross necklace that matched the one she had on. "To remind us that Jesus is the One who deserves our cheers and all the glory," she said.

Our half-time performance was flawless, even the grand-finale lift. I jumped into my stance with Breana beneath me as my secure base. I posed on her shoulders and smiled for the flash of my father's camera.

It was this picture of us that Breana had signed.

One afternoon after football practice, Drew Paterson caught up with us and asked me to the homecoming dance. My brain didn't know how to talk to Drew Paterson. I could only nod. His blue eyes alone were enough to leave me speechless.

Breana was the one who finally answered, "She'd love to!"

The night of the dance, Breana helped me do my hair and makeup and then left me with a hug. "Look for the heart. I'll be waiting up."

The heart. We had made those hearts for each other so many Valentine's Days ago that I don't remember when we started hanging them in our bedroom windows as a signal to meet at the back-porch swing.

I shared everything with Breana after the first, second, and even third date. After that, I began to make up excuses. It was too late, or I was too tired. It wasn't like I was doing anything really wrong. It was just that I knew Breana wouldn't understand the kinds of parties I was going to and the people I was hanging out with. Why did I have to explain myself to her anyway?

That heart began to anger me. "Just grow up, Breana," I'd spit under my breath when I passed by her window after a night out with Drew.

Until last night, when I didn't just pass by her window, but nearly passed out under it. I was losing my balance and then there was Breana, cradling my head in her lap, her cross pendant shining in the moonlight between us. Seeing it reminded me of who I was and who I belonged to. I reached up to touch where mine used to hang. How long had it been since I had thought to wear it?

Breana brushed my hair back out of my eyes.

"You are the real Miss Goody Two-shoes," I said and burst into tears.

That's what Drew had called me at the party. "A toast to Miss Goody Two-shoes. She's too good to drink with the rest of us sinners," he had said loud enough for everyone to hear.

My new friends lifted their drinks in mock salute. "To Saint Jeanine."

I laughed the hollow laugh that I had heard myself use so often the last four weeks. Then I grabbed Drew's drink and gulped it down. They all hooted their approval.

The alcohol's harshness shocked me. I couldn't breathe and when I finally gasped in air, I went into a coughing spasm. My stomach rolled. I needed help. I grabbed for Drew, but he dodged my reach.

"I guess some people just can't handle their liquor." He pointed at me, and they all snickered. Standing in the center of their ridicule, I suddenly wanted nothing more than to be the person they were accusing me of being.

These were my new friends? They laughed *with* me if I did what they did, but *at* me if I didn't.

"Please, Drew, I want to go home."

"Sure thing," he said, much to my relief. He wasn't such a bad guy. Tomorrow I would talk to him. I knew I could make him understand about his friends and these parties. After all, he had said that he loved me.

Drew took my hand and led me out the door to the sidewalk. He turned me towards home. "Go play with your dolls. Call me when you grow up."

I stumbled six blocks toward home. It wasn't until I saw the heart in Breana's window that I knew I had made it. I had made it back to home and back to myself.

The next morning came fresh and new, but just a little too early for me. I struggled to get out of bed and cleaned up for the day. This time I didn't forget to put on my cross. Faith renewed, I fastened the chain with a sense of purpose. I was starting over.

I flung open my curtains and hung my old Valentine's heart in the window. I wanted it to be the first thing Breana saw this morning. I could hardly wait for our reunion on the back-porch swing, to be together again.

Looking across at her bedroom, I almost expected to see Breana smiling over at me. The last thing I expected to see is what I saw. The heart was gone. Her window was empty.

I walked through the house and out to our swing in a fog of shock. There the shock turned to pain. On the swing cushion was half of the heart from her window. Breana had written just two words, *The End.*

I sank into the swing as torn apart as the heart I held on my lap. I reached up and touched my cross. It had taken me too long to see the truth. I was too late.

"I see you're wearing your cross again." I looked up at Breana standing over me. I wiped my tears and nodded.

"Jeanine, you know that Jesus restores the brokenhearted. And He can restore our friendship."

"Yes, Breana, I believe that."

Breana sat down. She placed the other half of the heart beside the one in my lap. On it were the words *Friends To.*

I studied the pieced-together heart for a moment before grasping what it meant. Hope started to fill me and I looked over to Breana.

"Friends to the end?" I finally managed to ask.

"Yes," Breana smiled and gave the swing a little push start with her foot. "Friends to the end."

FROM VICTIM TO VICTOR

BETTY LOEPPKY

We know that all that happens to us is working for our good if we love God and are fitting into his plans.

ROMANS 8:28 TLB

"OUR DILEMMA IS THAT WE HATE CHANGE AND LOVE IT AT THE SAME TIME; WHAT WE REALLY WANT IS FOR THINGS TO REMAIN THE SAME BUT GET BETTER."

Sydney J. Harris

The night was very dark. I found it hard to sleep. It was quiet except for the hum of the car motor, but after several hours, the car pulled to a stop. We kids were scrunched up in the backseat of the car, all of us sleeping except me. With my eyes shut and my ears open, I heard my mom ask, "Which way, left or right? Where do we go?" We were heading down the road with no destination.

Although my parents had hardly any possessions, they did have lots of "baggage." The car had room enough to carry seven restless kids, two adults, and every problem accumulated in my parents' dozen years of marriage. And each problem came with a forwarding address. Soon after our move, each problem took on a life of its own and began multiplying. The drinking problem became alcoholism; and anger grew into rage, producing a home filled with violence, fear, abuse, and a spirit of despair. There was lots of control, but no power to change.

At nights, my eyes would be closed, but my ears were always open. Constantly having to listen to the screams, the drunken arguing, and the physical fights drove me into a valley of hopelessness. We were all prisoners without choices or hope for change. As a teen I contemplated running away, but I feared it would take me down a path worse than the one I was walking. I thought of suicide, but my mind had no assurance or peace that the life hereafter would be any better.

In my early teen years, I lived across the street from a classmate at school. Her home was different than mine. After dinner at my house, my father would reach for a bottle. At her home after dinner, her father would reach for a Bible.

I had never before known a Christian family. I decided that my family was the way we were because my father was an alcoholic. It made sense to me that her family must be the way they were because her father was a Christian.

By the time I turned eighteen, I was determined to change my life. I wanted to be in control. I had longed for the time when I could make my own choices, so when I was invited to live with my cousin in another province, I chose to leave home without hesitation. My first Sunday away from home, I attended church. I heard from Romans 8:28 that God had a plan for my life, regardless of how out of control things might appear. I learned that God had "called" me for a special plan according to His purpose. I looked at my life, and I could see no evidence of a "plan." Although I never had personal contact with God, I certainly believed that He existed. And I wondered if my search to be in control was headed in the way of God's plan and call on my life. Could He turn all the horrible things in my life into something He could use for good? It seemed that I hadn't been able to turn my life around on my own. So I thought, *Why not let Him have control?*

After a few weeks, a new friend offered me an opportunity to make my destiny certain. Without a doubt, I wanted change. I wanted a new life. My friend explained that only God could give me the life I had been searching for—and only through His Son, Jesus Christ, could anyone receive it. I prayed, inviting Christ to be my personal Savior and Lord. That day I found the power to change. Real power for real change.

The darkness lifted from my life, and for the first time I felt a deep joy, peace, and hope. I felt like I had finally something to live for. Of course I did. God had a plan for me. I recalled Romans 8:28, and it suddenly became clear to me. If God could forgive and heal the pain in my life, then I could forgive those who had caused that pain. Through the power of Christ, I was able to completely free myself from bitterness and anger. That one decision gave me the power to change from being a victim to a victor.

That power to change has never lost its intensity. Over time, God's power has changed the junk in my life into jewels. He took the victim and made her a victor. My destiny is now one of hope and expectancy—a journey of joy as I walk with Jesus in His power and in His victory. I've found real power for real change for now and eternity.

GUNS 'N' PRAYER

TOM C.

(as told to Muriel Larson)

The just shall live by faith.

ROMANS 1:17

"What are you doing to my brother?" screamed the teenaged girl running into the street.

"I'm going to kill him, and now I'll have to kill you too!" I cried.

I had recently been released from prison after serving time for manslaughter. But I couldn't seem to stay out of trouble.

While living at a halfway house, I had gotten into a fight with a man.

The next morning I bought a gun, loaded it, and headed to the man's house. When he answered the door, I lunged in and grabbed him by the collar. Pulling him into the deserted street, I shoved him to the ground, jabbed a foot onto his throat, and took aim.

That's when the teenaged girl ran into the street. She fell to her knees and bowed her head.

Her posture startled me, but I held on to my victim and cocked the gun. As I debated which one of them to shoot first, I heard the girl praying.

Dear Lord, she said softly, *this man must be the most miserable person in the whole world. I pray that You will save him and give him the happiness he must be searching for.*

I stared at her. She wasn't praying for herself. She wasn't praying for her brother. She was praying for *me!*

My hand began shaking, and I loosened my finger on the trigger. Releasing the man, I walked over to the girl and handed her the gun. "Take this thing and throw it away," I mumbled.

Back at the halfway house, I threw myself onto my bed. The girl's prayer kept replaying in my mind.

I tried to get a hold of myself. I hadn't broken once during my long years in prison; now I was out, and I didn't want to turn soft. Yet this was the second time in just a few days that something had gotten to me.

Recently Gene, a counselor, had come to my room to talk to me about starting my life over again. I had let Gene talk for a while and then interrupted.

"Hey, Gene," I said, "I know you're interested in me. I think you really want to help me. But you—or anybody else—don't mean a thing to me. If I thought you were a threat to me, I'd kill you." I reached under my pillow and pulled out a hatchet.

Gene's face turned pale.

"But I know you're not here to hurt me," I admitted.

"Then give me the hatchet," Gene said. He breathed deeply when I handed the weapon over. "Do you know what your problem is, Tom?" he asked.

"What's my problem?" I mocked.

"You don't know the peace and love and joy of God." I knew his words were true.

"You're lost in your sins," Gene went on. "If you died tonight, you'd be lost forever. You need Christ as your Savior."

Gene looked at me for a moment. "You've never known real happiness, have you, Tom?"

"No, I haven't," I agreed.

"Well, why don't you receive Jesus as your Savior right now? You will find peace and joy."

I shook my head. "I'm not ready." I was glad when Gene finally left.

I had felt smug about my coolness then, but now...after that girl's prayer...

"Gene!" Later I shouted, opening his door. "Somebody get Gene! I've got to see him."

"I went out to kill someone this morning," I said, when Gene appeared. "I was ready to pull the trigger when his sister came out. I told her that I had to kill her too. Then she fell to her knees and started praying for me! Not for herself or her brother, but for *me!*"

I was too choked up to go on.

"That girl loved you, Tom," Gene said, "because she's experienced the love of Christ. She wasn't afraid to die. She was concerned about your soul. That's why she prayed for you."

I nodded in agreement.

"Tom," Gene said softly, "are you ready now to accept what Jesus did for you on the cross? He can give you the same peace and faith that that girl has."

The battle was over.

"Yes," I replied. "I'm ready."

As we knelt in prayer, I experienced peace in my heart—a peace I had never known before.

My whole attitude changed when I received Christ into my life. Instead of wanting to hurt people, I wanted to help them. As I got into the Bible, I learned more about Jesus Christ; and He not only gave me peace—He gave me understanding.

I have since become manager of the halfway house. The Lord has enabled me to help other men fresh out of prison to start new lives, as I did. I know the problems they're facing. I also know the only certain Help for them.

But I wouldn't be serving there today if it hadn't been for a teenage girl's timely prayer.

FREEDOM BEHIND BARS

NEELY ARRINGTON

"I was in prison and you came to visit me."

MATTHEW 25:36 NIV

My stomach tightened in a knot as the iron door slammed shut behind me. I never dreamed I'd be in a place like this. The guard ordered us to walk, hands behind our backs, to the end of the hall.

"Turn left," he shouted.

Rounding the corner, I heard a noise that sounded like three gunshots...*bam, bam, bam.* I jumped, grabbing the hand of the girl beside me. At the same moment, she screamed. Turning, I saw eyes peering through a tiny window in the lock-down cell next to me. The mouth that belonged to those eyes yelled a barrage of the foulest language I've ever heard.

The offensive verbal assault continued as the cell door was punched and kicked. I've never been so scared. ——

The guard motioned for us to go on. Walking down the hall, I couldn't help but think how angry and afraid that prisoner must be behind bars. I had fears of my own, but I was here to try to make a difference for people just like these prisoners. I was here to minister.

When preparing for the prison-ministry choir tour, I didn't know what to expect. We spent countless hours learning songs, choreography, and speaking roles in order to present the Gospel of Jesus Christ to prisoners. When the week finally arrived, we visited ten juvenile detention centers in Florida. We left each with a different story.

On the surface, our first experience seemed like a disaster. It was pouring rain when we arrived, and we were forced to cancel our outdoor performance. Instead, we squeezed into a tiny meeting room. There was not enough space to set up all the risers and sound equipment. As we started the performance, we felt uneasy because we were so close to the prisoners. We totally blew the first song, messed up the choreography, missed our cues, and forgot our lines. The prisoners mocked us and made fun of our dancing. I was unprepared for their hostility. Only a few of the inmates really seemed to be listening.

From the very beginning, one girl in the back row caught my eye. She watched me as I sang and danced, and she tried to sing along with me. When our pastor began to talk, she started weeping, and I knew God was speaking directly to her. During the invitation, she raised her hand, saying she wanted to accept Christ. It broke my heart to think a girl who seemed so sweet had to live her life in prison. Leaving the room, I glanced her way and she mouthed "Thank you." That was the only thing that let me know that even though everything else seemed to go wrong, God still worked in spite of our mistakes.

In another prison, we were allowed to interact with the inmates. Following the performance, the superintendent let a few girls from the choir talk to the female inmates. We only had fifteen minutes, but we made the most of it. Even though these girls were behind bars, it didn't take me long to realize that they were like me. They had hopes and dreams, fears and frustrations. The only difference was the wrong choices that had brought them to this point in their lives.

One girl had a baby she had only seen a few times. She struggled with a drug problem and asked us to pray that the Lord would take the cravings away from her. She was to be released the next day. That afternoon she made a decision to follow Christ. If we had been at that prison one day later, she wouldn't have heard us. She might never have accepted Jesus Christ as her Savior. I saw that God was in control and His timing was perfect.

There were other ways I saw God at work. One of the chaperones was an interpreter for the deaf. We never expected her to need to interpret on the trip, but in one of the prisons, she saw a boy with something in his ear. She learned from a guard that the boy was deaf, and there was no one at the prison to interpret for him. She was given permission to do so, and he never took his eyes off her. During our invitation, he accepted Christ. If she hadn't been with us, he might never have "heard" the Gospel.

Probably the most intense experience occurred in our ninth prison visit. Our performance seemed to be going well, but suddenly a young boy sitting right in the middle of the inmates got sick and vomited all over the floor and himself. The prisoners sitting around him began to laugh and make fun of him. A guard came and led him out of the room, and three others came to clean up the mess. I knew it was getting close to the important part of the service, so I prayed that God would keep the inmates focused.

As our pastor began speaking, it was obvious he had the attention of the whole crowd. At every prison he basically gave the same message, but that day he spoke with greater emphasis and his words seemed to have more power. As I listened, I looked across the sea of faces and saw a boy who looked like he was about sixteen or seventeen. He was weeping so much and so openly that a guard brought him a towel to wipe his tears.

A boy in our group got permission to talk to the crying teen. The inmate told him that for a long time he had known who God was, but was confused about Jesus and didn't know what to believe. Watching us and listening to the pastor speak cleared up all his questions. He finally understood who Jesus was and what the message of salvation was all about. He was so thankful we had come. He joyfully accepted Christ.

We all continued to be concerned about the young boy who had been ill. Our pastor and his son went to the infirmary to see him. They told him how much they cared about him and how much Jesus loved him. Our pastor watched prayerfully as his son led this boy to Christ.

There are so many more stories to tell, but these stand out among them. Over and over we saw God at work. We saw angry, lonely, hopeless teenagers come to understand and respond to the good news of Jesus Christ. Although I know we touched the lives of many prisoners, our lives were changed too. We came home with a new sense of thankfulness for our blessings and our freedom in Christ.

Most of those prisoners are still behind bars, but because of God's grace and our ministry among them, many now have a personal relationship with Jesus Christ. They are experiencing freedom behind bars.

THERE'S ALWAYS A WAY OUT

TAMEKIA REECE

Have I not commanded you? Be strong and courageous.
Do not be terrified; do not be discouraged, for the
Lord your God will be with you wherever you go.

J O S H U A 1 : 9 N I V

Tears streamed down the face in the mirror. *How did things get this bad?* I looked down at the tiny blue pills cupped in the palm of my hand. *Should I do it? What other choice is there? Is death my only option?*

"Larry, I don't want to be with you anymore."

"What," he snapped, his head whipping around to face me.

"I think we should see other people," I said softly, my eyes focused on the floor.

I flinched when he jumped up and came over to me, yanking my hair back, forcing me to look up at him. "You will never leave me," he shouted, his spit flying into my face. "The only way you're leaving me is in a casket!" With that, he shoved me and walked out the room. Slumping to the floor, I cried.

After the first insult, I should've been gone, but of course I stayed. After all, I was only fifteen and in love for the first time. When he said he was sorry and would never do it again, I believed him, hoping things would change. Instead things only got worse. What had started out as a few demeaning comments had turned into slaps ever so often. From the slaps came shoves and punches and with each one my self-esteem was shattered a little more.

Filled with insecurity, I started to believe every word he said. Not believing things would ever get better, wanting to leave, but afraid he'd make good on his threats, I felt there was only one way out—suicide.

Night after night, I lay in my bed, contemplating killing myself. *How would I do it?* I knew a gun or a knife would be too painful—perhaps a drug overdose was the way to go.

Gripping the pills in my hand, tears flowed down my face. I shook uncontrollably, watching my reflection in the mirror doing the same. I wasn't ready to die; I just wanted the beatings to stop, the pain to go away. I wished that there was a way to turn my life around. I needed help, but I had no one to turn to. No one understood what I was going through. I had no other choice.

As I placed the first pill in my mouth, it hit me—there *was* Someone to whom I could turn.

Letting the pills hit the floor, I dropped to my knees, bowed my head, and cried out to God. Choking through my sobs, I begged Him to give me the strength and courage to get out of that relationship, to keep me safe, and to watch over me. Guilt-ridden, I asked Him to forgive me for what I had almost done. My cheeks drenched, I finally went to my room and cried myself to sleep.

When I awoke the next morning, a great rush of relief washed over me. I had never appreciated just how beautiful it is to actually wake up each morning. I knew that God was watching over me and would guide me through this—I had a second chance at life and I was going to make the best of it.

That day, I left my "boyfriend" and never looked back—finding I was happier than I had been in years. Although I felt a little guilty and even shameful about considering suicide, I realize that God forgave me and I should forgive myself. With His help and guidance, I have found that there is truly no problem in the world, no matter how big it may seem at the time, that can't be fixed. With a little perseverance and faith in God, there is always a way out.

SMILEY

KAREN MAJORIS-GARRISON

Freely you have received, freely give.

MATTHEW 10:8 NKJV

"EXTENDING YOUR HAND IS EXTENDING YOURSELF."

Rod McKuen

I was in the prima donna, self-centered age of seventeen, and my motives were simple—to enhance my final grade in Health Assistant class. To accomplish this goal, I decided to volunteer at the nearby convalescent center.

For weeks I grumbled to my boyfriend. "I can't believe I'm stuck taking care of old people for free!" He agreed. The bright yellow uniforms my classmates and I were required to wear made matters even worse. On our first day at the center, the nurses took one look at our sunshiny apparel and nicknamed us "The Yellow Birds."

During my scheduled days, I complained to the other "yellow birds" how emptying bedpans, changing soiled linens, and spoon-feeding pureed foods to mumbling mouths were not jobs any teenager should have to do.

A tedious month passed, and then I met Lily. I was given a tray of food and told to take it to her room. Her bright blue eyes appraised me as I entered, and I soon became aware of the kindness that rested behind them. After talking with her for a few minutes, I realized why I hadn't noticed Lily before, although I had been past her room numerous times. Lily, unlike so many of the other residents, was soft-spoken and undemanding. My first day at the convalescent home, I discovered the staff had their favorite patients—usually those with character that stood out in some way. From joke tellers to singers, the louder and more rambunctious the patient, the more attention he or she received.

Something inside of me immediately liked Lily, and strangely, I even began to enjoy our talks during my visits to her room. It didn't take long for me to realize that Lily's genuine kindness stemmed from her relationship with God.

"Come here," she said and smiled to me one rainy afternoon. "Sit down. I have something to show you." She lifted a small photo album and began to turn the pages. "This was my Albert. See him there? Such a handsome man." Her voice softened even more as she pointed to a pretty, little girl sitting on top of a fence. "And that was our darling Emmy when she was eight years old."

A drop of wetness splattered on the plastic cover and I quickly turned to Lily. Her eyes were filled with tears. "What is it?" I whispered, covering her hand with my own.

She didn't answer right away, but as she turned the pages I noticed that Emmy was not in any other photographs. "She died from cancer that year," Lily told me. "She'd been in and out of hospitals most of her life, but that year she went home to Jesus."

"I'm so sorry," I said.

"It's okay," she smiled slightly, meeting my eyes. "God is good to those who love Him, and He has a plan for every life, Karen. We need to open our hearts to Him whether we understand His ways or not. Only then can we find true peace." She turned to the last page. Inside the worn album was one more picture of a middle-aged Lily standing on tiptoes and kissing a clown's cheek.

"That's my Albert," she laughed, recalling happier memories. "After Emmy died, we decided to do something to help the children at the hospitals. We'd been so disturbed by the dismal surroundings while Emmy was hospitalized." Lily went on to explain how Albert decided to become "Smiley the Clown."

"Emmy was always smiling, even in the worst of times. So I scraped together what fabric I could find and sewed this costume for Albert." She clasped her hands in joy. "The children loved it! Every weekend, we volunteered at the hospitals to bring smiles and gifts to the children."

"But you were so poor! How did you manage that?" I asked in amazement.

"Well," she grinned, "smiles are *free,* and the gifts weren't anything fancy." She closed the album and leaned back against her pillows. "Sometimes the local bakers donated goodies, or when we were really hurting for money, we'd take a litter of pups from our farm. The children loved petting them. After Albert died, I noticed how faded and worn the costume was, so I rented one and dressed as Smiley myself; that is...until my first heart attack, about ten years ago."

When I left Lily's room that day, I couldn't think of anything other than how generous she and Albert had been to children who weren't even their own.

Graduation day neared, and on my last day of volunteer services at the ward, I hurried to Lily's room. She was asleep, curled into a fetal position from stomach discomfort. I stroked her brow, worrying about who would care for her the way I did. She didn't have any family, and most of the staff neglected her except for her basic needs, which were met with polite abruptness. At times, I wanted to proclaim Lily's virtues to the staff, but she'd stop me, reminding me that the good things she'd done in life were done without thoughts of self. "Besides," she would say, "doesn't the good Lord tell us to store our treasures in heaven and not on this earth?"

Lily must have sensed my inner torment above her bed that day as she opened her eyes and touched my hand. "What is it, dear?" she asked, her voice concerned and laced with pain.

"I'll be back in two weeks," I told her, explaining about my high-school graduation. "And then I'll visit you every day. I promise."

She sighed and squeezed my fingers. "I can't wait for you to tell me all about it."

Two weeks later, I rushed back to the center, bubbling with excitement and anxious to share with Lily the news of my graduation events. With a bouquet of lilies in my hand, I stepped into her clean, neat, but unoccupied room. The bed was made and as I searched for an answer to Lily's whereabouts, my heart already knew the answer.

I threw the flowers on the bed and wept.

A nurse gently touched my shoulder. "Were you one of the yellow birds?" she asked. "Is your name Karen?" I nodded and she handed me a gift-wrapped box. "Lily wanted you to have this. We've had it since she died because we didn't know how to get in touch with you."

It was her photo album. Written on the inside cover was the scripture Jeremiah 29:11 NIV: "'For I know the plans I have for you,' declares the Lord, 'plans to prosper you and not to harm you, plans to give you hope and a future.'" I clutched it to my chest and departed.

Three weeks later, my horrified boyfriend stood before me. "You can't be serious!" he said, pacing back and forth. "You look ridiculous."

We were in my bedroom and as I tried to view myself in the mirror, he blocked my reflection. "You can't be serious," he repeated. "How in the world did you pay for that thing anyway?"

"With my graduation money," I answered.

"Your what?" he exclaimed, shaking his head. "You spent the money that we saved for New York on *that?*"

"Yep," I replied, stringing on my rubber nose. "Life should be more about giving than receiving."

"This is just great," he muttered, helping me tie the back of the costume. "And what am I supposed to tell someone when they ask me my girlfriend's name? That it's Bozo?"

I looked at my watch. I needed to hurry if I wanted to make it on time to the children's hospital.

"Nope," I answered, kissing him quickly on the cheek. "Tell them it's Smiley...Smiley the Clown."

THE RUNAWAY

MYRA LANGLEY JOHNSON

By wisdom a house is built, and through understanding it is established.

PROVERBS 24:3 NIV

The note on the front seat of the bus read, "Pastor Paul, I've run away for good. Don't try to find me because you never will. Love, Melissa."

To break up the long bus trip home from a national youth gathering, the church youth group had stopped for an evening of fun at Six Flags Over Texas in Arlington. The bus had been parked out front since late afternoon. It was now 10:30 P.M., and neither Pastor Paul nor the sponsors had any idea how long Melissa had been gone. Her friends reported not having seen her for hours.

Fighting their rising panic, the pastor and youth sponsors immediately placed calls to the airport, train station, and bus depot, but no one recalled seeing a fifteen-year-old fitting

Melissa's description. She had vanished. The group prayed and cried together before confronting the awful task of calling Melissa's mother to relay the devastating news. Their arrival home the next day—returning with one less youth than they had when they left—was met with stunned sorrow. The parents waiting for the bus all had tears in their eyes.

What no one knew was that Melissa had been planning her escape long before the youth trip began. She had already emptied her savings account, and on the day they arrived at Six Flags, she had secretly packed a small knapsack with necessities, carrying it with her as they left the bus. Entering the park, she chatted casually with some friends while they decided which ride to try first. Shortly after they got into line for one of the rides, she suddenly announced, "Hey, guys, I really need to go to the bathroom. Have fun. I'll catch up with you later."

Instead she made her way to the exit, took a taxi to the bus depot, and headed west toward San Diego, where her father, a police officer, had relocated following his divorce from Melissa's mother. Nervous about traveling so far on her own, she planned her nights to be on the bus and avoid the danger of sleeping in strange places. She arrived in Phoenix the next day and called Kelly, an old friend in that city, saying she'd left the youth trip early to join her father in San Diego.

"Mom's such a perfectionist," she explained, "expecting me to be in everything and do everything, and I'm tired of the constant pressure. I know things will be better with Dad." She led Kelly to believe the arrangements had all been cleared with her parents. In truth, Melissa felt her mother couldn't possibly understand how burdened and confused she felt, and the only solution she could think of was to run away. Surely once she moved in with Dad, everything would be all right. Melissa attended church with Kelly's family on Sunday, swallowing the discomfort she felt at lying to her friend and feeling like a hypocrite as she tried to participate in the worship service. She could only pray that God was watching over her and would somehow make things turn out all right.

Later that afternoon, she caught the overnight bus to San Diego, but when she arrived Monday morning, more doubts surfaced. *Can I really trust my father to take me in, or will he blow up in anger over all the worry I've caused everyone and ship me back to Mom?* "I may have really messed up," she confided to Donna, a young Christian woman she had met on the bus. "Now I don't know what I should do."

"Why don't you stay with me for a couple of nights until you figure it out? My roommate just moved out of our apartment, so there's plenty of room." Donna squeezed Melissa's hand. "Besides, I'm a great listener. Maybe I can help you sort things out."

"Thanks, that would be great," Melissa said, brushing away a tear. But days later, even with Donna's support and prayers, she still hadn't found the courage to contact her father.

With her savings quickly running out, she applied for a job at a nearby McDonald's, never anticipating that during the company's routine reference check, the manager would actually phone the drive-in where she had once worked back home. In her close-knit community, it didn't take long for the news to be passed to her mother. Finally, one terrifying week after Melissa's disappearance, her worried mom had confirmation that her daughter was alive and safe.

That week Melissa celebrated her sixteenth birthday…alone. Although Donna had proved to be a patient and understanding friend, she was still a stranger. Melissa remained completely out of touch with her family. With each passing day, she realized more fully how much she loved and needed them, but the longer she waited to make contact, the harder it became. She dreaded the inevitable confrontation once she picked up the phone to call. She began to doubt that even God could forgive her for what she had done to her family.

Melissa did her best to ignore the loneliness welling up inside. Her job at McDonald's at least gave her something to do to pass the time and earn a little cash. Lunch hour was one of the busiest times, and she had grown accustomed to the regular appearance of the neighborhood police officers stopping in for burgers and fries. She hardly noticed one day when a different policeman stepped up to the counter. "Can I help you?" she asked, barely glancing up.

Then her eyes met his, and she found herself staring into her father's surprised gaze.

"Melissa?"

"Dad! I—"

At first Melissa's dad was speechless, after a few moments he found his voice and began to talk. His tone conveyed more relief than anger. It was a miracle, he said, finding her like this, because the neighborhood wasn't his usual beat. "God must have brought me here, Honey. I'm so glad I found you. I'm so glad you're okay."

Melissa couldn't wait to rush from behind the counter and accept his welcoming embrace. *This must be what the Prodigal Son felt like,* she thought, recalling the parable from the Bible. Her father convinced her to come home with him, and before long he had made arrangements for her mother to fly to San Diego so they could talk things out.

When at last she and her mother sat down together, they came to realize how each had failed to communicate her own needs and feelings. "I just assumed you wanted to be involved in all those activities," Mom said.

"I thought I had to for you to be proud of me," Melissa replied. "It felt like you were pushing me to do things I really didn't care about."

Their tearful discussions finally led to solutions. Other than the typical required studies, Melissa's mom agreed to let her decide what activities to be involved in and how often. Melissa agreed to family counseling and training sessions in communication skills. Three weeks from the day she ran away, Melissa returned home to begin her junior year of high school.

Melissa has since graduated from college, earning her law degree, and now practices family law. Her goal is to keep parents and children in communication and really listening to each other and maintaining the type of relationship God intended them to have. "When I ran away," Melissa told Pastor Paul later, "I had no idea I could talk to my mom and that she would listen, and my mom had no idea how unhappy I was with my life. When you love someone, you have to talk, no matter what. And you have to forgive. When you do—when you really begin to understand what's going on with the other person—that feels *very good*."

SHE LOVED CHILDREN

ROBIN BAYNE

And God shall wipe away all tears from their eyes; and there shall be no more death, neither sorrow, nor crying, neither shall there be any more pain: for the former things are passed away.

R E V E L A T I O N   2 1 : 4

"I can't believe we're here, for this," I whispered, shaking my head. I touched my younger sister's hand, giving her a gentle squeeze for comfort.

My mother and I exchanged pained glances, knowing no easy answers would come to us. Our entire family gathered now with the mourners, all of us pulling together even more tightly than usual. No one we called "friend" had ever been taken from us like this before.

We were surrounded by flowers—mostly white, some pink— all giving off that sweet smell often associated with weddings and funerals. I could taste the salt from my own tears, and felt

GOD SHALL BE MY HOPE, MY STAY, MY GUIDE, AND LANTERN TO MY FEET

William Shakespeare

how heavy my eyelids had grown. My sister's sixteen-year-old best friend had just died, leaving behind a crowd of stricken family and friends.

Among the photos on display was my favorite, one of Dawn walking in the snow, holding the hand of another little girl, a cherub-faced toddler. Dawn had always loved little children, and had enjoyed babysitting.

I can still recall the ticking clock in the living room where we had gathered to wait and pray.

Dawn had been the focus of her mother's life, as the family had been torn apart by divorce. Gathered together once again, for a bitter reason, Dawn's estranged parents embraced to comfort each other. Who would have ever imagined they would come together again for such a sad reason?

We all exchanged greetings and condolences, amid much nose-blowing. We shared anecdotes followed by tight, forced smiles. Some of the stories were funny, but the chuckles were laced with tears.

Her mother confessed feeling terrible about forcing Dawn to practice her typing for an hour before going out that evening, the one that turned out to be her last.

Adding to my own pain was the knowledge that I'd never really gotten along with Dawn. I'd always thought of her as an annoying teenager like my own little sister, and now it was too late. I said a silent prayer hoping that up in Heaven, Dawn understood how I felt.

One story I couldn't share that night was about the time Dawn joined us on a family camping trip, and spent most of the time being a little brat. Or so we thought. We were celebrating my father's birthday, and she had hung back, not participating. When we sang over a lit birthday cake, Dawn had pushed back into the corner, pouting. We all thought it was strange, and tried to encourage her to join in our fun. She chose not to, and my family began to wonder if bringing outside friends along on trips was a good idea for the future.

Did she resent the attention focused on someone other than her? We had no idea. It wasn't until much later that we learned how upset Dawn had felt because her own divided family would never again celebrate the way that we were. Nothing had been the same since her parents had divorced. She told my sister she'd felt lonely, watching the happiness we shared. I thought of all the photographs around my house, with their images of a happy family—mom, dad, my sister, and me. The tragedy of her death reminded me of how much I had to be thankful for, of how many blessings God had given me.

After the funeral, life went on much as before, although our house was more quiet, my sister's room in particular. Little things we used to worry over now seemed trivial in comparison to the reality of life and death. Dawn's mother spent many hours with my mother before suddenly moving away, perhaps to make a fresh start, perhaps to escape the constant reminders she saw in my sister.

Healing began for all of us, as time passed, and I still think about her spending that last hour of typing practice before climbing into a car with three other teens. Were they speeding? Had they been drinking? I realize that none of that matters now, but I remember how my little sister and I matured after the experience.

"You know," my mother said one day, about a year after the funeral. "Someone I know told me she believes Dawn is up in Heaven, helping greet the little children as they arrive."

I thought of that photograph taken years before, of Dawn and the little girl, surrounded by pure, white snow. I can't imagine a better job God could find for a teenage angel.

ADOPTED FOR A PURPOSE

LYNDELL ENNS

For I am not ashamed of the gospel of Christ: for it is the power of God unto salvation to every one that believeth.

ROMANS 1:16

I was just three months old when my parents adopted me. I am told that lying in a motel dresser drawer that very first night, I looked up at my new parents with distrust and suspicion, as if to say, "You just try to control me!" My mischievious streak was obvious from day one, but incredibly, I was now in a home where firm and loving parents would put me in touch with my Maker.

Thanks to my new family, I wasn't very old at all before I understood that life is precious. After that comes an eternity in one of two places, Heaven or Hell. It was easy enough to decide which was the better place. When I learned that receiving Christ was the only way to Heaven, I knelt with my father, and asked Jesus to forgive my sins and give me eternal life.——

"THAT WE ARE ALIVE TODAY IS PROOF POSITIVE THAT GOD HAS SOMETHING FOR US TO DO."

Lindsay

I lived smugly in the safety of this newfound "fire insurance," because that was all Christianity was to me at that point, until a certain question began to haunt me: *What is the purpose of life?* It haunted me because the only answer I had carried alarming implications. I began to believe that life was basically meaningless. What are we here for anyway—to live, make babies, and then die? Simply perpetuating the human race did not appeal to me. Nor was I interested in chasing after material riches only to leave them behind in seventy years. There just wasn't a good reason for living anymore. Nothing I could do was going to matter in a hundred years anyway, much less for eternity.

But when I was fourteen, I learned at a summer Bible Camp that there *was* a purpose for my life. It came from God. After all, He'd made me, so who would know better than Him what that purpose is? I also learned that God had created me to relate personally with Him, to know Him, and to love Him. And, that completely giving my life over to God for His purpose was the key to an abundant and meaningful life. Suddenly, my life had purpose and significance. I was created to know God and to glorify Him for eternity.

It was only minutes after realizing my purpose that I also discovered the plan that would bring eternal significance to my life. I was to share the truth and meaning that I had found in Christ with others. I realized that showing people the way to

Christ helps to change their destiny for eternity, just like my adopted parents had helped to change *my* eternal destiny.

My nature is to be selfish and proud, so I have a natural tendency to continually try and take the steering wheel of my life away from Christ. Inevitably, that's about the time I end up in a ditch or down a blind alley. Thankfully, He is always forgiving, and graciously resumes control when I give Him back the wheel. In my life, Christ has replaced the meaningless races and goals I could be chasing in this world with eternal purpose and significance.

Christ also wants to give you life in all of its fullness. With Jesus, you can find the meaningful life you were meant to have.

THE "P.K."

JACOB P.

(as told to T. Suzanne Eller)

**Now make confession to the Lord, the
God of your fathers, and do his will.**

EZRA 10:11 NIV

I have been a P. K. (pastor's kid) from the time I was born. I
spent a lot of time playing in the halls of my dad's church as I
grew up.

When my mom brought me home from the hospital, my older
brother took one look at me and said, "So when are you taking
him back?" Maybe he knew what he was talking about, because
I turned out to be quite a rowdy kid for a preacher's son! I'll
never forget when I was in the Christmas pageant. My part was
to play a shepherd. When I came out onto the stage, I held the
sheep on my head and kept it there the whole show. I'd do
anything to get a laugh.

"A MAN
MAY GO TO
HEAVEN
WITHOUT
HEALTH,
WITHOUT
RICHES,
WITHOUT
HONORS,
WITHOUT
LEARNING,
WITHOUT
FRIENDS,
BUT HE
CAN NEVER
GO THERE
WITHOUT
CHRIST."

John Dyer

When I went to school, I hesitated when people asked me what my dad did. It wasn't that I didn't like the fact that my dad was a pastor, but it was hard when the kids at school would mock my family, God, and me. I almost became ashamed of what my dad did. I wanted people to accept me for who I was, not just as a preacher's kid.

School was hard for me. I liked girls from a very young age. It's interesting how even little kids can make each other feel rejected and hurt.

So, it was decided that we would try homeschooling. My mom and I didn't really click during that time. I was always fighting with her about what I was supposed to do. Because of my attitude, I was grounded for most of the time that I was homeschooled. It wasn't all bad. Sometimes my mom and I really hit it off and were close, but two years later I decided to go back to public school.

This time I was determined it would be different. I dressed in baggy clothes and bleached my hair. I started to hang out with people who accepted me for who I was instead of labeling me as a P. K. Though they lived and acted very different from my beliefs, they allowed me to be myself.

Music opened the door to more opportunities for me. I loved music of all kinds, but most of all I loved listening to and playing the drums. I was a natural, so my parents gave me a drum set for a birthday gift, and I started taking private lessons from a professional. My initial goal was to play in a worship band and to eventually play professionally. But when I joined the jazz band at school, people were impressed with my ability. Then I received an offer to play in a punk band. I wasn't really all that thrilled with the whole punk scene, but I stayed in it because playing in a band brought me attention and popularity. And I started sacrificing my values in order to gain more acceptance.

We performed for the high-school talent show, and the audience loved our band, the "Burnouts." Then we started playing at parties, which could often be pretty wild. In fact, the police even had to shut down a few. At this point, I was in full-blown rebellion against God, and I knew it. I liked my new life, and yet I still felt this certain emptiness that wouldn't go away. But I was struggling with the desire for the acceptance from my peers—that I had worked so hard to earn.

During this time my family and I took a trip to Alaska to see my cousin. I attended a church with their family one night. When I walked into the youth group, I was astonished to see how freely everyone worshiped God. These teens didn't seem to care what people thought of them. As I watched them worship, it hit me that God was actually in that room. I felt Him there. Away from everything and everybody, away from home, I could now clearly see that God loved me with His whole being—not as a P. K., but for who I really was on the inside.

I bowed my head with a knowledge deep inside that I needed to deal with some issues. That night I opened my heart and gave my personal struggle with rejection and acceptance from others to God, and He deeply touched my heart.

When I arrived home, I made a decision to quit my band. That was the hardest thing I've ever done. I called our guitar player and told him that God had changed my heart. When I lost my position in the band, I also lost my girlfriend. It hurt, but it was easy to see that she had fallen for Jacob the drummer, not Jacob, the person. The losses continued as so-called friends walked away, people who had only liked me because I was connected to the band.

But then I changed my focus. I began telling people at school how God had given me a deep sense of purpose. I shared my story with one of my best friends who later got so hooked on the Word of God that he now knows more about the Bible than I do. And then I met a really special girl. Today, we are both striving to follow what God wants for us together, but also what He wants for us as individuals.

I still play the drums, but now I'm playing for my church worship team. I am writing and one day I plan on leading my own worship team.

Now I don't fear what people think or say when they ask me what my dad does. I am proud of my heritage and I am proud of who I am. I look them straight in the eye and explain that my dad is a pastor.

In fact, I plan to be just like him in a few years.

TRIGGER

NIKKI D.

(as told to T. Suzanne Eller)

Those who are wise will shine like the brightness of the heavens, and those who lead many to righteousness, like the stars for ever and ever.

DANIEL 12:3 NIV

A few years ago my gang made national news when we went to war with a rival gang. I lost fifty-three friends that summer. Dodging for cover whenever a car slowed down near me became a part of life. Sometimes I didn't have time to duck, so I crossed my arms in front of my chest and hoped the impending bullet would miss my heart.

I was in state custody for most of my childhood. When I was released at the age of seventeen, I was a time bomb waiting to explode. I immediately joined a gang and began selling drugs. I had been doing drugs from the age of seven, but soon after I was let out on the streets, my habit was so bad that I sometimes woke up in some unknown hallway, unsure of how I got there.

My whole aim during this time was to excel in my gang, and I did. I planned to be the female president for my block. However, despite the money, drugs, and my friends, I was still miserable. I remember standing across the street from a church and watching as the Christians left the building. They looked happy, and I wished that one of them would tell me what made them so content. I wanted to know how to smile. But no one who came out of the church ever spoke to me. I'm sure it was because of the angry front I presented.

Suicide was on my mind all of the time, and I hated my life. I wanted answers, but wasn't sure how to find them.

Then one day two Christians knocked on my door. I was happy to see them, but I certainly didn't let them know that. At first, I tried to slam the door in their faces. One young lady put her foot in the door, and I thought, *She doesn't know my name is "Trigger."* Yet, privately, I admired her boldness.

I asked them tough questions, thinking I could shake them. "Share your views on premarital sex," I demanded. They answered. I continued to fling questions at them. "Show me where God said, 'Thou shall not smoke weed,'" I said. "Didn't God say the earth and fruit of it were ours?" They answered my questions one by one, and I shot back with more. "How do you know that Christianity is the truth and that other gods are not?"

They told me about Jesus. I challenged them further. "What color or nationality is Jesus then? How can this God of yours relate to a black, inner-city girl like me? What does your God have to do with the people I live among every day?"

One of the ladies looked at me, and she stopped me before I could ask another question. "Nikki, you can come up with all of the excuses and questions that you want, but I want to ask you a question: When you die, where will you be then?" Her voice was gentle. "You know what I'm afraid of? That you'll be lost, without hope, and without Christ."

That got my attention and somehow, deep down, I knew they were telling the truth to me. I knew I didn't want to die the same way that I lived and I reached out with my heart and I accepted Christ right there on my front doorstep.

Immediately I began telling everyone about my decision to follow Christ and the new happiness I had found. Before long, I was preaching on the street corner. For the first time in my life the void was filled, and I wanted to tell everyone! I had tried Allah, therapy, hypnosis, alcohol, and drugs—and finally, I had found something that was real. My relationship with Christ filled the void that had been in my heart my entire life.—

It is a miracle how God helped me to walk away from my old lifestyle.

One day while I stood on the street corner witnessing, one of my former fellow gang members stood a few feet away, watching. She had come to ridicule me. As she came closer, she asked me about this new game that I was playing. When she saw that I was serious and didn't ignore her or try to make her leave, she stopped ridiculing me and started listening. I told her about Jesus and what He had done for me, and she broke down in tears, sobbing. I had the privilege of leading her to Christ that day.

Since then, I've traveled with my church on short-term mission trips. I've been in several foreign countries, but my primary mission field remains the streets of New York.

Before I leave home each day I ask God to show me who needs to hear about Him that day. Once I arrive, I pray for people to respond to what I am saying. I meet people who are from other religions who have questions about my faith. Others still sometimes mock or ridicule me. But most genuinely want to know about God and how to know Him. Some ask me to pray that God will help them with their problems. Many accept Christ as we stand on the street corner and pray.

Every day I pray for Christians to understand the need to share their faith in God with people like me. There were

Christians who never once walked across the street when I stood outside their church, hoping. But I'm thankful for those who finally, boldly walked up to my door to share with a hurting person in need. Their obedience to God changed my life.

MISSING PIECES

LEE EZELL

**You made all the delicate, inner parts of my body, and
knit them together in my mother's womb.... You saw me
before I was born and scheduled each day of my life
before I began to breathe.... How precious it is, Lord,
to realize that you are thinking about me constantly!**

PSALM 139:13,16-17 TLB

Many people have what I call a "missing piece" in their
lives—holes in their past, as if something has been punched out.
I understand what that is like.

I was born and raised in Philadelphia's inner city feeling
hopeless and unwanted. Both my mother and father were
alcoholics. The police showed up regularly to our house in
response to domestic violence calls.

God? He had always seemed like an absentee Owner to me.

Then one day as a teenager, I stumbled into a religious meeting advertised in the newspaper. The speaker was Billy Graham. As he shared about God, I made a simple surrender of my life to God. The One who had always seemed "out there somewhere" became real and present in my life.

Soon, I graduated from high school and moved to San Francisco, where I got my first job. I had not worked in that office long when a salesman I met at work one morning, cornered me that night and brutally raped me.

When I finally escaped, I sat in my car on the side of the road crying my eyes out. *"Why, God? Why me?"* I cried. I remember thinking, *This is the story of your life, kid. You are a loser.*

I made the very poor decision that night in not calling the police or telling anyone what happened. *It's all over,* I thought. *I just need to toughen up.*

But I was emotionally and physically ill for weeks. I finally went to the doctor. "You don't have the flu," he said. "You're pregnant."

It took me three days to summon the courage to tell my mother. "You'll have to take care of this problem," she said. "I can't handle it. Come back when it's over."

I got in my little Volkswagen and drove down California's coast toward Los Angeles, not even sure where I'd wind up.

I remember flipping through a Bible left by the Gideons in an old, dirty motel room and coming across Psalm 139. King David was speaking to God, saying, "You made all the delicate, inner parts of my body, and knit them together in my mother's womb…. You were there while I was being formed in utter seclusion! You saw me before I was born and scheduled each day of my life before I began to breathe" (vv. 13,15-16 TLB).

Maybe I was an unwanted child, I thought, *but apparently God created my life with meaning and for a purpose.* If this verse was true, I realized, then there are no illegitimate children, including the one who was growing inside of me.

That moment of truth helped me make a decision to let my child live and place her up for adoption. Months later I gave birth to a tiny baby girl.

I never got to see or hold my precious little girl and this became a huge missing piece of my life. But I have since learned that God is truly the Holder and Protector of missing pieces. When I met my "prince" a few years later, he came riding along with two children in the saddle. He knew about missing pieces, too. He had lost two wives—one to a brain tumor and another to a rare blood disease.

A few years later, I was sitting at home when the phone rang. The voice on the other end said, "Hello. My name is Julie. You've never met me, but you're my mother." She said she had two reasons for calling: to tell me that I was a grandmother and to lead me to Christ. How wonderful it was to share with her that she herself had already done that many years before!

Julie had learned about the rape years before and had been depressed, confused, and angry until she visited her minister, who showed her Psalm 139. *If this is true,* she had decided, *then God wanted me to be born.*

She is now a lovely young lady with a family of her own and living proof that God is faithful. He does not forget. He hasn't lost my address—or yours. He's able to make something beautiful out of the things that are not. The challenge for us is to place the missing pieces in His capable hands and let Him fill up the gaps in our lives.

DAD, I LOVE YOU

(as told to Christy Sterner)

Above all, love each other deeply,

because love covers a multitude of sins.

1 PETER 4:8 NIV

I had a lot of anger in my life. It wasn't something outwardly manifested, but there was a kind of inward grinding. I was disgusted with people, with things, with issues. Like so many other people, I was insecure. Every time I met someone different from me, he became a threat to me.

But I held an anger and hatred for one man more than anyone else in the world. My father. He was the town alcoholic. If you're from a small town and one of your parents is an alcoholic, you know what I'm talking about. Everybody knows. My friends would come to high school and make jokes about my father being downtown. They didn't think it bothered me. I was like other people, laughing on the outside, but you can be assured, I was crying on the inside.

I'd seen my mother beaten so badly she couldn't get up. When we had friends coming over, I would actually take my father out, tie him up in the barn, and park the car up around the silo—telling friends he'd had to go somewhere. I don't think anyone could have hated anyone more than I hated my father.

Just before leaving to go to college I made a decision to follow Christ. It was in the months following that a special love from God entered my life and was so strong it took my hatred and turned it upside down. After years of resentment, I was at last, able to look my father squarely in the eyes and say, "Dad, I love you." And really mean it.

When I transferred to a private university I was in a serious car accident. My neck in traction, and I had to be taken home. I'll never forget my father coming into my room. He asked me, "Son, how can you love a father like me?" I said, "Dad, six months ago I despised you." Then I shared with him my decision to follow Christ: "Dad, I let Christ come into my life. I can't explain it completely but as a result of that relationship I've found the capacity to love and accept not only you, but other people just the way they are."

Forty-five minutes later, one of the greatest joys of my life occurred. Someone in my own family, someone who knew me so well I couldn't pull the wool over his eyes, said to me, "Son, if God can do in my life what I've seen Him do in yours, then I want to give Him the opportunity." Right there my father prayed with me and asked God to be a part of his life.

Even though my dad has gone on to be with the Lord, I am so thankful for the assurance of knowing that one day, I will be reunited with him in Heaven.

HOPE WHEN LIFE'S TOUGH

MIKE "PINBALL" CLEMONS

Let us hold unswervingly to the hope we profess,

for he who promised is faithful.

HEBREWS 10:23 NIV

"WHEN
YOU SAY
A PERSON
OR A
SITUATION IS
'HOPELESS,'
YOU ARE
SLAMMING
THE DOOR
IN THE FACE
OF GOD."

Charles L. Allen

Growing up in the housing projects of Dunedin, Florida was tough. We lived right down from the railroad tracks, across from a sewage treatment plant—every negative stereotype you can imagine. But amazingly throughout my childhood I never realized we were poor, because there was always so much love and acceptance in my life. I wouldn't trade my childhood for anything.

My mom was only eighteen when she had me, and I grew up without a father. There were times when my dad promised to come by and bring over things for Christmas and for my birthday, but then he would never come. I always tried to make sure I didn't show any disappointment because I didn't want to hurt my mom. I never wanted her to think that she was insufficient. And I can't say I would have turned out better with my dad around.

Mom was more than I needed. Too many times you have parents who are doing well financially, but they give all they have to their careers. My mom gave all that she had to me, and she supported me in anything that I did. She also gave me a foundation in the church, a belief system so that when I left home I had something to hold on to.

In the South, they say you go from the hospital straight to the front of the church. There was a time when I went to church because I had to. But when I accepted Jesus into my heart at the age of nine, it became more of a personal decision.

Because of my relationship with Jesus, I've always been encouraged, even in challenging times. People often remember comments made throughout their lives, "My mom used to say this all the time," or, "My dad used to say that all of the time." Well, my mom used to say, "Stop smiling all the time." It seems I always had this big grin on my face, and she used to ask, "What's that smile for?" It was because I had Jesus in my heart.

But I've had my share of tough times. When I got older, I was told I wasn't smart enough to go to college and I was too small to play football. But after four scholarship years at the College of William and Mary, I signed with the Toronto Argonauts. I've been with the CFL ever since.

I've had personal struggles as well. My great-great grandmother, whom I loved deeply, passed away before she could see me succeed as a football player. My wife's father was shot and killed when we were in college. Her sister died of cancer only three weeks after discovering she was ill—leaving behind three small children, one of whom lives with us now. Most recently, my wife's mom died.

Everyone has trials. No one is exempt. The difference is having a hope in Jesus Christ. One thing that makes me sad is when I see people with no hope. That really bothers me. But I understand it perfectly, because apart from God, there is no hope. If we don't put our hope in God, then we are putting it in things that perish and fade away.

There are a lot of things we could complain about, but sometimes it is through the hard times that we learn how to touch the lives of others. I discovered early in life that God is the only way to complete happiness. By giving my life over to Him, I've learned the true purpose and meaning of life. God is in control, and I'm comfortable with that.

SURGE OF COURAGE

LISA ALLEN

(as told to Esther M. Bailey)

You will receive power when the Holy Spirit comes on you; and you will be my witnesses...to the ends of the earth.

ACTS 1:8 NIV

As I packed for a mission trip to Tijuana, Mexico, I tried to squelch the nagging fear that threatened to mar my adventure. Surely God wouldn't want me to ruin my first trip out of the country with concern about how hard it was for me to witness, would He?

During orientation, the leader emphasized spending time with God in preparation. I prayed that I would be an effective witness with my words, as well as with my actions.

But every time my faith began to take hold, I would be reminded of previous failures. I had just finished my junior year of high school. During that year, I had finally decided to make my

Christianity known. And the locker room of the girls' basketball team on which I played seemed the ideal place to start.

"Would you like for me to say a prayer before the game?" I timidly asked the other girls.

With the shrug of her shoulders, one girl said, "It couldn't hurt." The others showed little interest.

Dismayed by the lack of enthusiasm, I said in a weak voice, *God, be with our team and help us to be unified. Protect us from injury. Amen.* I remembered the incident with shame. If I couldn't do better than that in Mexico, I might as well stay home.

By the time our group left for Tijuana, I knew that I would participate in a drama.

Without words, only through props and action, the drama portrayed the crucifixion and resurrection of Jesus. *Witnessing made easy,* I thought. But that was before we performed in Juvenile Hall.

About fifty guys there had committed crimes ranging from theft to murder. During our drama, the lewd looks and vulgar comments of the men made me feel cheap. We weren't reaching them with the gospel at all—I could tell.

When our actor playing Jesus came on the scene, however, the mood of the men changed. They even sobered during the portrayal of Christ being beaten and crucified, and they seemed touched by our invitation to begin a new life. In their situations, they must have realized how much they needed a second chance.

After the drama, a Spanish interpreter explained God's plan of salvation and asked the men to come forward if they wanted to accept Jesus as their Savior. At first no one moved; then two boys came forward. Before long about twenty guys joined them. No doubt some of them came forward out of peer pressure and others merely wanted to be close to the girls. Still, if only one life was changed in that place, our endeavor was worthwhile.

For me, another visit—the visit to the orphanage—was heart-rending, yet rewarding at the same time. It hurt to see so many children starving for love with no one to love them. Still, I found joy in bringing them happiness, if only for a few hours. After we had finished our drama and a puppet show performed by other members of my group, we took the children to buy ice cream at a nearby store.

With the little Spanish I knew, I talked with a couple of girls on the way. When one of them saw the boy who played the part of Jesus in our drama, she asked me to tell him to stay with them. Pointing to her heart, I said, *"Jesus vivirá en el corazón,"* which means, "Jesus will live in your heart." When she smiled and grabbed my hand, I hoped she understood.

By the time we went to T. J. Revelation Street, I thought I had become adapted to the culture, but I was unprepared for the

"Red Zone." As we passed out tracts to prostitutes and homeless people on the street, I felt like I was standing at the very gate of hell! Drunks stumbled out of the clubs blaspheming God's name.

While we enacted our drama, people rudely walked through the scenes, yelling and laughing at us. But we kept our focus on God and did not allow the interruptions to distract us.

During the drama I noticed a tall, tough-looking guy who would have frightened me had I been alone. Afterward, he came up to talk with me and a couple of my friends. Between his few words of English and the Spanish I knew, I learned that he had some religious knowledge. He was tired of the way he was living and wanted an experience with God.

If I had been in a similar situation at home I would have enlisted my pastor to lead this man to Christ. But there, I was the only one who knew enough Spanish to even talk with him.

Suddenly I felt what seemed like a surge of courage from somewhere inside of me. Without hesitation, I began to instruct and pray with him. *"Gracias, gracias,"* he said when we finished. We then gave him a Bible in hopes that it would help him understand further his new life as a Christian.

When I returned to school in the fall, I made a personal vow to myself to try and be a stronger Christian example to those around me.

I started inviting my friends to church. In the locker room I led our prayers with more confidence, asking God to help us make the best use of our abilities, not for ourselves, but for His glory.

Then, before one game someone else led in prayer; so I remained silent. To my surprise, one of the girls said, "Lisa, we'd like you to pray too." I knew then that this newfound courage God had placed in me and a little help from the Holy Spirit, was strong enough to touch the lives of others and make a real difference.

A CROSS ON THE MOON

COLLEEN WHEELER

**There is salvation in no one else! Under all heaven there
is no other name for men to call upon to save them.**

ACTS 4:12 TLB

Coming home from the airport, I felt embarrassed. Here I was
hung over from drinking too much, with nothing but a little
black dog and what I carried in my duffel bag. I had wanted to
get married and have a child, but instead I was back in New
York, dragging a small black dog on a leash behind me.

I had grown up in a multicultural neighborhood in the
suburbs of New York. My parents were on-and-off-again
alcoholics. As the oldest of six children, I became the one
everyone leaned on for support, which meant I cleaned,
shopped, cooked, and changed the diapers. Suffering a lack of
parental support growing up, I was left emotionally craving love
and attention.

"HE WHO
PROVIDES
FOR THIS
LIFE, BUT
TAKES NO
CARE FOR
ETERNITY,
IS WISE
FOR A
MOMENT,
BUT A FOOL
FOREVER."

John Tillotson

By the time I was sixteen, I'd had enough. I gave up trying to be the responsible one and instead started drinking and smoking. I was soon caught up in my own cycle of addiction. Nothing mattered, except to try and escape from my circumstances.

Deciding I could make some quick money, I moved to California to become an actress. Instead, I ended up a statistic, dancing in a bar. Although it was degrading, I acted as if I didn't care.

Eventually, I tried to pull my life together and pursue my dream of acting. I took some acting courses, but my constant drinking led to dropping out of school and then to living with a man I thought I loved. We traveled up and down the coast, selling second-hand goods at swap meets. When we didn't travel, we marketed drugs. It was a terrible existence.

One time, after a drinking binge, my boyfriend beat me up. I didn't have the resources to make it on my own, and decided my only other option was to take my little black dog and go back home to my parents.

I stayed with them for a year and started working in a hair salon. Then, with the help of an Alcoholics Anonymous program, I started to live a sober lifestyle.

A year later I became critically ill with hepatitis B, to the point that I almost died. One of my clients from the salon invited me to attend church, telling me that I could receive prayer for my illness there. I went, and at the end of the service, I prayed to accept Jesus into my heart. I continued to go to church for a few months, but despite the vividness of my conversion experience, I struggled with ill-fated decisions on my life's journey.

Eventually, I married an independent filmmaker, thinking he could make all my dreams come true. But after our first movie together, our marriage became a nightmare. Having married for all the wrong reasons our marriage naturally had no strength on which to stand and we ultimately divorced.

All of these struggles caused me to pull away from God. But then one night, a strong wind blew through my window, and into my room. When I got up to fix the blinds, I saw what appeared to be a huge shadow of a cross overlaying the moon. Awestruck with the awesomeness of God, I instantly dropped to my knees, asking Jesus to forgive me for my sins.

Jesus has since placed in me a burning desire to tell others about Him. I'm currently on staff part-time in my church and attending Bible school, pursuing a degree in theology. I'm also still working part-time as a hairdresser in the entertainment industry. As for my acting ambitions, I've put them in God's hands and know that I can trust Him to use me for the life purpose for which He designed and created me.

A CASUAL WITNESS

MATT LUTZ

(as told to Esther M. Bailey)

We are therefore Christ's ambassadors, as though

God were making his appeal through us.

2 CORINTHIANS 5:20 NIV

When I said yes to stay over on a Friday night, I didn't exactly have sharing my faith in mind. I merely wanted to have fun with three cool guys.

Chris, Joey, and Jason were my new friends at school. Friendship with guys who were not Christians was new to me because I had hung around Christians for most of my life. These guys seemed to have their heads on straight, though, so I decided to step out of my usual circle.

The evening got off to a carefree start: plenty of soda to guzzle, pizza to scarf, and jokes to tell, followed by an intense Nintendo challenge. I was having a blast.

But the moment Jason's parents headed off to a movie the good, clean fun came to a halt, and trouble raised its ugly head. Jason dragged out one of his dad's *Playboy* magazines, held it up, and grinned. "Okay, gentlemen," he said. "It's time for some *real* fun."

Chris and Joey tried to act cool, but I thought they seemed a little edgy too. My heart skipped a few beats, and I was nervous, but I knew I had to take a stand. I wasn't afraid of being shot down because I figured I might as well find out if these guys were my true friends or not.

"Jason, I'm not so sure this is right," I said. Actually, I was *positive* the magazine was off-limits, but I didn't want to come on too strong.

"It's okay, Matt—really, it's no big deal," Jason said. "I look at this stuff all the time."

"Don't worry. We won't tell," Joey added.

I slumped back on the couch, wondering how to explain. "It isn't that," I finally said. "I don't want to fill my head with that kind of stuff."

The guys' strange expressions were filled with a million questions, so I sat up and continued. "Sure, looking at *Playboy* seems fun. But we've got to be careful if we don't want to get messed up for life."

The room grew still and the guys just stared in disbelief. "I think it'd be better if I don't stay," I said as I jumped to my feet. "I'll just go call my mom to come get me."

When I dialed our number from the phone in the kitchen, I got a busy signal. I tried a few more times and then gave up. I peeked into the family room, expecting the guys to be freaked out with the *Playboy.* But the magazine was nowhere in sight, and the guys seemed to be in a serious mood.

Jason met me in the doorway with a soda. "Matt, we've been talking," he said with a reddened face. "We don't want you to leave. Okay?"

Chris chimed in. "Yeah, we're sorry. We didn't mean to make you feel uneasy."

"Let's just forget what happened and get on with the fun," Joey said as he looked down at the floor.

I glanced around to meet each face with a smile. "Deal."

We all jumped into another action-packed Nintendo challenge, but the mood wasn't crazy like before. Everyone was still a bit edgy. Just when I was about to crack a joke to put some life back into the party, Chris spoke up. "I don't get it," he said. "What is it that makes you so—you know—different?"

Yikes! That question had only one answer. I gulped and plunged right in. "I'm a Christian," I said.

As I tried to explain my faith, I soon found myself in a deep discussion about Christianity—deeper than I really ever considered taking the conversation.

"Would you happen to have a Bible in the house?" I asked.

Jason pulled out a dusty old Bible that was hidden at the back of a shelf. I didn't know quite where to begin, but I did the best I could to explain the miraculous birth of Jesus and why He died on the cross.

"Being a Christian isn't just following a set of rules," I said. "It's having a relationship with Jesus. That happens when you ask Jesus to forgive your sins and you turn your life over to Him."

Before long, the time seemed right to ask the ultimate question: "Would you guys like to accept Jesus as your Savior?"

All three nodded. We stood in a circle and I explained how they should pray and then suggested they pray in their own words. Joey did.

After the prayer, Joey said, "Matt, it was really weird. Before we prayed, I seemed to be under a lot of pressure. But when I asked God to forgive my sins, it felt like a heavy load fell off my shoulders."

Wow! I wondered if I was in an unchurched home or at a testimony meeting! I had heard others say things like that, but I was so young when I asked Jesus to come into my heart that I hadn't really felt like I'd been carrying a load of sin.

The experience of leading my friends to Christ was absolutely awesome! I couldn't believe how everything happened so naturally.

Although I moved from Phoenix to North Carolina a week after that night, I asked my church friends to keep in touch with my new Christian brothers, and I trust the Holy Spirit to do the rest.

I LEARNED THE TRUTH AT SEVENTEEN

TONYA RUIZ

For the Lord does not see as man sees; for man looks at the outward appearance, but the Lord looks at the heart.

1 SAMUEL 16:7 NKJV

"I learned the truth at seventeen that love was meant for beauty queens...." Those words spilled from our car radio in 1975, and I believed them. As a scrawny twelve-year-old, I believed that if I were beautiful, my life would be perfect.

Four years later at age sixteen, I was chosen from more than 200 girls to go to Paris and become a fashion model. My agent told me, "Your rail-thin body, shiny blond hair, and sky blue eyes will be your passport to success!" *Teen* magazine wrote an article about my life called, "A Model's Success Story: It's like something that happens in the movies!"

My "glamorous" and "exciting" life was filled with dancing, drinking, dating, and parties. Life was a thrill a minute. It never occurred to me that my excessive eating and drinking could affect how I looked, but it did. At the modeling agency one day, I was told, "You look puffy and tired!"

At a photo shoot the hairstylist painstakingly arranged my hair in an elegant upsweep. I put on a gown that was waiting for me. The assistants set the lighting, and I settled into position. Then the photographer scrutinized me up and down, and said, "No. No good. You can go home." My first taste of rejection as a model was devastating—I felt as if I had been punched in the stomach. On the way home, I purchased a huge chocolate bar and overindulged.

Six months later, I was living on my own, in an apartment in New York. One evening, my mom called. "Your agent, Valerie, called us and said you've gained a lot of weight. She said you're fat. Tonya, are you fat?"

"Yes!" I cried. "And I look horrible!"

At sixteen years old, I had a whopping 120 pounds on my 5 foot 7 inch frame. That was ten more pounds than I weighed in the fabulous pictures that filled my modeling portfolio. The traitorous pounds that made my face look puffy were keeping me from my dream of becoming a supermodel.

Every time I stepped on the scale it was torture. By any normal person's standards, I would have been considered thin, but not by the fashion industry's standards and certainly *not* by the standards of my New York agent, Eileen Ford. After a weeklong fast, I walked into the agency and said, "Eileen, look. I've lost weight!" I weighed 118 pounds. She looked me over and said bluntly, "You're still fat—lose five more pounds."

My eating habits were out of control. The more I tried to lose weight, the more I ate. I bought Haagen Dazs ice cream and consoled myself with it. I would eat an entire box of Frosted Flakes and a gallon of ice cream at one sitting. Then I would take a handful of laxatives. I sat with my head over a toilet trying to make myself vomit. I took diet pills to help me lose weight, speed up my system, and diuretics to rid myself of unwanted water. I wanted to look perfect, but my eating habits continued to spin out of control and so did my life. I could only be as happy as I was thin.

My looks consumed me. I was obsessed with food. When I scrutinized my appearance, I saw myself through a fun-house mirror. My view was distorted—what was real was not what I saw. Somewhere along the way, I had lost sight of what was true. When I looked in the mirror, I no longer saw the image of someone like Cheryl Ladd, but of Miss Piggy. My value, both to

myself and to my agents, was in the way I looked, and since I
could not look "perfect," I felt worthless.

During the next two years, I traveled 75,000 miles as a
fashion model. I used food, alcohol, drugs, and men to try to fill
an empty place in my life. The glamour and excitement of my life
wore off quickly. I explored various churches and New Age
philosophies, read self-help books, and consulted my horoscope
daily—searching for answers, but I didn't find any. My weight
roller-coastered from high to low, as did my emotions. At the
ripe old age of eighteen—when most young girls would have
just graduated from high school and were just beginning their
lives—I concluded that my life was over. Suicide seemed to be
my only option. I flew home from Switzerland to say good-bye to
my family before I killed myself.

Soon after I reached home, a friend of mine called and invited
me to church. The pastor asked, "Do you have a void in your
life? Have you tried everything, but still feel empty?" It felt as
though he was speaking directly to me. He shared about the
Lord and how to receive His salvation. I ran forward, knelt down,
and accepted the Lord that night, and my life took a new
direction. My heart filled to overflowing. God healed me—
physically and emotionally.

Ten years later, I attended a ladies' event at my church. My
husband stayed home with our four young children. During the

message, the speaker recalled: "I took my teenage daughters to Disneyland. While we were waiting in line, I asked them to look around at the crowd and pick out a woman that they thought was beautiful. They couldn't find one."

As soon as I got home, I sat down in front of my computer and began writing about a life I hadn't talked about in years. I wondered, *Can I teach my children to see themselves through God's eyes?* I didn't want them to compare themselves with the media's impossible standards of beauty they saw on commercials, billboards, and magazine covers all around them. Would they realize that their worth to God was not measured by their weight or contingent upon high-chiseled cheekbones? How would I balance that message with the fact that they should take good care of the unique and wonderful bodies God created for them? As I tucked their sweet, pajama-clad bodies into bed that night, I read them a verse from First Samuel: *For the Lord does not see as man sees; for man looks at the outward appearance, but the Lord looks at the heart* (16:7 NKJV).

Over the years, I have encouraged my children to be beautiful—on the inside. My grown daughters now attend Bible College. They've been to Europe too—but as missionaries, not fashion models. My two sons grow taller by the day.

Recently, I awoke during the night, unable to sleep. It was cold outside, but I was warm in my cozy bed as I lay next to my husband. With his arm draped across my body, he was so close that I could feel his heartbeat and his warm breath upon my face. I was filled with peace and contentment. Had I taken my life in that lonely hotel room twenty-two years ago, I would have missed all of this.

I still struggle sometimes with wanting to look younger and thinner. I wish that my stomach did not lie next to me when I sleep on my side! Fortunately, I know that physical beauty is only skin-deep and temporary, and that true beauty is soul deep. God accepts me regardless the size of my jeans, the condition of my skin, or my reflection in a mirror. He loves me so much that He sent His only Son to die for me. And I am, indeed, valuable to Him.

IT'S YOUR CHOICE

"G."

(as told to T. Suzanne Eller)

I have set before you life and death,

blessing and cursing; therefore choose life.

DEUTERONOMY 30:19

"IT IS NEVER TOO EARLY TO DECIDE FOR CHRIST, BUT THE DAY WILL COME WHEN IT WILL BE TOO LATE."

Anonymous

Colin was not happy to be where he was at the moment. At the age of sixteen, he had ended up in a facility for troubled children and teens, which severely restricted his ability to do his own thing. He was an extremely intelligent young man, but he had made some incredibly poor choices. Some of those choices should have cost him his life, but amazingly, he was still alive. Well, maybe it would be better to say he was alive on the outside. On the inside, he was nearly dead. He was one hurting kid, and he was going to force everyone around him to pay for the pain he was experiencing.

That's where I came into the picture. Twice a month it was my privilege to load up the keyboard and amplifier and head for

"The Mountain" (the nickname for Colin's new home). My purpose was to share the love of God with those kids who had come from all walks of life and were thrown together under one roof. It's rather ironic that society takes a hurting teenager from a dysfunctional setting, crowds him into a facility with lots of other hurting, dysfunctional teens, and then wonders why these kids can't get along with each other.

In all fairness, though, I must tell you that "The Mountain" was a bit different than many other group homes nationwide. Even though it wasn't openly touted as a Christian organization, the administrators were moved with compassion to minister to the spiritual needs of the kids, as well as their physical needs. Every Wednesday night a *Faith and Life* session was made available for voluntary participation by any resident youth who chose to come. Since these meetings were the only opportunities for boys and girls to see each other, frequently the attendance was large, for that fact alone. In other words, not everyone who came to *Faith and Life* was there strictly for spiritual edification!

That was the case with Colin on the very first night I met him at "The Mountain." He wasn't really interested in his spiritual condition. He was interested in a certain girl. The only problem was that this particular girl did not come to the meeting that night. So Colin was now stuck at a Christian meeting for a couple of hours, where he *definitely* didn't want to be! He made that very clear through most of the service by stirring up agitated chaos in his area of the circle.

I'll never forget what I felt led to teach that night. It was about choices. I brought two sets of car keys with me to the meeting and two jars of fairly clear liquid. Early in the session, I held up both keys, one in my right hand and one in my left, carefully hiding the lower part of each key, so no one could determine what type of vehicle each key started. I instructed the kids to individually pick one of the keys in their own mind, without having any knowledge at all about either of the keys.

Then I did the same with the jars of liquid. Holding one in my right hand, and one in my left, I asked them to each make a choice silently, without knowing anything about the substances in the jars. After a few seconds, I placed the jars and the keys back into my bag and proceeded to teach the kids about choices. I explained to them that some people make a choice about Jesus, whether to accept or reject Him, based on absolutely no knowledge about Him at all.

During the most powerful part of the message, Colin suddenly raised his hand and waved it around to be sure he got my attention. His timing was inappropriate, and I was not at a point to really address questions. But something compelled me to respond to Colin's insistence. I acknowledged him and asked what he wanted to say.

He blurted out, "I just want you to know that I don't believe any of this. I don't believe in God. I don't believe in Jesus. I don't believe in the devil, and I don't believe in hell." Then he shut his mouth as quickly as he had opened it and watched for my reaction.

Without missing a beat, I heard myself calmly respond to Colin, "Well, then you've made your choice, haven't you?" I picked right back up where I'd left off in my message and continued on as though there had never been any interruption.

Near the end of the presentation, I reached down into the bag and pulled out both keys again. This time when I held them up exactly like before, I explained what type of vehicle each key operated. "The key in my left hand starts a Ford truck, and the key in my right hand starts a Honda Accord. Maybe you're a little disappointed with your original decision now, but remember, you had absolutely no information to help you make an informed choice. And besides, it probably doesn't make a whole lot of difference which key you picked. The type of car you drive is not usually a life or death matter."

Then, laying the keys aside, I reached into the bag and brought out the two jars of liquid again. "But *this* is a different matter!" I exclaimed, holding the jars up as before. "If you had come in from outdoors on a hot day and picked up this jar to drink," I said, holding up the jar in my left hand, "you would be perfectly safe, because it only contains water with a few drops of iced tea."

"However," I cautioned, "if you had gotten a drink from the other jar, you would have been seriously injured and possibly could have died, because that jar contains water with bleach. It looks exactly like the first jar, but its contents would have begun eating away at your throat and esophagus immediately." I paused for a few moments to let that truth soak in.

Then I proceeded, "Without proper information about the contents in those jars, you could have made an uninformed decision that cost you your life. This was definitely a life or death matter!"

After a momentary pause, I continued, "There's another life or death matter about which every person comes to face at the crossroads of life. It's the choice about whether to trust Jesus and let Him come into your life. Unfortunately, many people make this decision with very little or no information, so they shut the door on the one Person who can free them from their guilt and pain. Today, I'm here, to give you the information you need. Jesus is the best friend you'll ever have. He said He'd never leave you or forsake you, even though others might. He took all your sin, so He could give you His righteousness. This, too, is a life or death matter. If you choose Jesus, you get life!" ——

At that point, you could have heard a pin drop. Each one of those kids was looking deep inside to examine their own heart. That's when I invited them to open up their heart to give Jesus a home in their life.

Guess who the first person was with his hand in the air to make Jesus the Lord of his life. Exactly!! *Colin!!* This hurting young man who had caused such a distraction in his area of the circle all night, who had disrupted the message with arrogance and disgust earlier, was now making a wonderful choice. He was choosing life!

Others followed suit, and I led them all in prayer to receive the free gift of salvation through belief in Jesus Christ.. There was a precious flow of the anointing of God, and afterward I hugged them each individually and welcomed them into the family of God. Then it was time for *Faith and Life* to end. But literal "faith" and "life" had just begun for many of those kids that night

When I returned two weeks later, I was greeted by one of the supervisors who asked to speak with me privately. We went to her office where she proceeded to tell me about the dramatic change that had taken place in Colin since the last time I was there. Colin had suddenly begun doing his schoolwork with such excellence that he had made straight *A*'s on every paper for the last two weeks. During this time, he had also begun to follow all the guidelines and obey all the rules with an exceptional attitude. This woman was so impressed with the turnaround in Colin's life that she couldn't wait to tell me the good news.

You see, Colin had stepped into the blessings of God because someone gave him the correct information, and he was able to *"choose life"!*

GO HOME, SARAH

SARAH CARMICHAEL

"For I know the plans I have for you," says the LORD.
"They are plans for good and not for disaster,
to give you a future and a hope."

JEREMIAH 29:11 NLT

As I walked through the front door and tossed my school books on the table, I heard my mom say my name. Normally, I would have headed straight to my room to avoid her drunken tirades, but my curiosity got the best of me, and I crept quietly down the hall towards the kitchen to better eavesdrop on this conversation. Mom's back was turned to me, but I could tell by her slurred speech and her unsteady swaying that she'd been drinking most of the afternoon.

That didn't surprise me. What totally shocked me were the words I heard coming out of my mother's mouth. Using terms that would make a grown man blush, my mom ranted and raved into the phone, describing my supposed immoral lifestyle.

Too stunned to even cry, I ran to my room.

Is that really what my own mother thinks of me?

Even though some of my friends had begun experimenting with sex and drugs, I still held fast to the moral standard I'd been raised with—saving myself until marriage. I didn't have a personal relationship with God, but I did have a good conscience and a high moral standard.

What my mom thought of me mattered a great deal too, and the wounds from her words went deep. It was hard enough being a "good kid" in a home where alcohol often turned my parents into irrational strangers, but to have my mom think—and speak—such terrible untruthful things about me.

It was a life-altering moment in my life. If she felt I was such a terrible person…then I would just live up to her expectations. And in my pain and disillusionment, I grimly determined that it hardly mattered that I was trying to be an upright person.

Years later, I found myself in a filthy apartment hungry and shivering under my thin shawl on a bare mattress, trying to pull my thoughts together.

At that moment, I heard the words: *Go home, child.* Then I heard the words again, clearly. I heard them with my heart.

Go home, Sarah.

I instinctively sensed that God was speaking to me, but vaguely wondered why He would tell me to go to the last place on earth I wanted to be. The cold forced me to get up and move, and that's when I first noticed that I was alone. The usual sprawl of unconscious people were missing, and as I stumbled about the filthy apartment, I realized that so were my stash, my drug money, and even my clothes. While I'd been sleeping off the drugs my so-called "friends" had taken everything I owned.

Only minutes later, I found myself standing in the rain, thumb out, hitching a ride toward home. I had nowhere else to go. Desperation and anxiety grew in my heart as each ride brought me closer to the explosive environment I'd once escaped. All too quickly, I found myself dropped off at a gas station just miles from my house.

Oh God, I don't want to go home—help me!

Only silence was returned. Despondent, I waited in the gray drizzle for the next car to stop. Soaked and shivering, I climbed into the Volkswagen bug that slowed and stopped a few yards past me. The driver was a young man with curly black hair and the kindest blue eyes I'd ever seen. He drove me the rest of the way home that day, but more importantly than that—he pointed me towards Heaven.

Along the way, he bought me lunch. After devouring the first real food I'd had in a long time, I found myself pouring my heart out to this total stranger, telling him why I'd run away and why I was even more afraid to go home. He listened quietly until I'd finished talking, then looked directly at me with his piercing eyes.

"Sarah," he said gently, "you are so precious to God. I've just met you, but I can sense your sweet spirit."

Before I could protest, he continued, "God has wonderful plans and a special purpose for your life, and as strange as this may sound, I believe the road to this new life begins by going home."

Go home, Sarah.

The words from earlier that day came echoing back to my heart. I felt an unexplainable peace—an assurance that everything would work out all right. Even though I had no clue how.

My new friend took me home that day, and I found my parents in worse shape than when I'd left. But God had a plan for me, and I was able to move right in with Christian relatives the following week. My aunt and uncle not only provided a stable home life for me, they took me to their little country church each Sunday. There I sat, week after week, listening to the amazing truth of God's love for me.

The words the young man had spoken to me began to bear fruit. I longed for a relationship with my loving, Heavenly Father, and wanted to know His plans and purposes for me. One Sunday, I found myself walking down the aisle and that very day

I left the church a new person in Christ. I'll never forget how I felt that day—every sin had been washed away! I was pure—I was clean. Forgiven for all I'd done.

And I'll never forget that young man who obeyed the Lord's prompting and spoke words of hope, encouragement, and strength to me.

I will be forever grateful.

Thank you for the ride. And for speaking words of life.

MISSY'S INSTINCT

BECKY WARNER

Don't let anyone think little of you because you are young.
Be their ideal; let them follow the way you teach and live.

1 TIMOTHY 4:12 TLB

On September 30, 1998, David Miller was returning to his home in Fayetteville, Arkansas, after spending several days in Minnesota on business. David suffered from severe back pain, often so excruciating that it would paralyze him, but the spinal specialists he'd consulted could offer no cure.

It was almost midnight, and two hours into his drive along a rural highway, when David's back began to spasm.

"My left leg started to cramp, and then I got a massive spasm," recalls David. "It just literally took my breath away...that's the last thing I remember." He lost control of his pickup truck, which then went over an embankment and crashed under a bridge. The next thing David knew, he was trapped in the dark beneath the wreckage, immobilized by pain—drifting in and out of consciousness.

"My first memory was looking out of the vehicle, and wondering why I was in a cave," says David. Paralyzed with pain, he prayed. I said, *Lord, I need help. I cannot move.*

Although the pain was unbearable, there was nothing David could do but wait and pray that someone would soon find him.

The next morning, a school bus was traveling the same route that David had taken the night before. On board, fourteen-year-old Missy Warner was thinking about the upcoming school day. As she gazed out the window, something caught her eye.

"It was a white truck. You could see a little bit of the windshield, and it was broken," recalls Missy.

Missy immediately sensed that something was wrong, but when she approached the bus driver and told him what she had seen, he refused to stop. His theory was that someone was probably just fishing down there.

"It didn't feel right, the truck sitting way down there…. I couldn't even see anybody down there fishing, and there was no road down there," says Missy. "And I thought nobody would really drive down there because they'd get stuck."

Once her school day began, Missy focused on her studies. She didn't think about the truck under the bridge again until that afternoon on the bus ride home. Coming from the opposite direction, however, the angle was not as good, and though she strained to see, Missy didn't have a good view of the spot.

"I was trying to look out the window, but it was too close to the side of the bridge that you couldn't see it," she explains. "I just thought I'd see it in the morning if it was down there."

Trapped beneath the bridge for over twelve hours now, David was having sharper back spasms than ever, compounded by injuries from the accident. David was in so much pain that most of the time, he wasn't even aware of the vehicles passing overhead.

"I was in and out of consciousness," says David. "I could remember trying to move one time but the pain was just too much, it was almost like I couldn't catch my breath, and I would pass out."

That afternoon, Missy tried to tell her mother, Becky Warner, what she'd seen.

"When she came home from school, she seemed kind of worried," Becky recalls. "She said, 'Mom, there's a truck down by the bridge.' She said, 'Don't you think we should look into it?'"

"I brushed it off," Becky admits. "I told her that somebody probably was fishing down by the bridge." Becky told her daughter that if she noticed the truck again the next day, then maybe they would talk about it.

"She wouldn't listen to me, nobody would," states Missy. "It made me mad, so I just went to my room."

Twenty-five miles down the highway, David's wife, Justine Miller grew increasingly worried about her husband. He was twenty-four hours overdue.

"My biggest fear, as time went on, was that they wouldn't find him alive," she stated.

Two of the Millers' sons had been out searching for David all day, without finding a trace of him. The airline confirmed that he had arrived on his flight from Minnesota, and a search of airport parking lots revealed that David's pickup had left the airport.

"The boys got to where they didn't really want to drive up in the driveway to look at the expression on my face," says Justine. "They'd look up at the door, and they'd put their heads down, and I knew then that they hadn't seen or heard anything."

That night, Justine prayed for the safety of her husband as she had never prayed before. "My time spent here was praying," she says, "asking God to please let the boys find him alive, that he would be okay."

That same night, Missy also said a prayer.

"I prayed for whoever was in the truck, that they would be okay until I could tell somebody who would listen to me and check it out."

But would her prayer be answered? And would anyone believe the intuition of a fourteen-year-old girl?

On the morning of Friday, October 2, Missy Warner crossed the bridge for the third time—hoping that the truck would be gone. But nothing had changed.

"Everything was the same. It was in the exact same spot, so I knew there was something wrong," recalls Missy. She pleaded again with the bus driver to pull over, but he told her that there was no safe place for the bus to stop.

That day at school, she tried to alert a teacher after class, but she says, "I don't think he believed me. You know, he just thought it was my imagination." Frustrated, she says, "It made me mad that nobody was listening."

Now having endured more than thirty-six hours without food or water, David was increasingly feeling the effects of hunger and dehydration.

"I prayed," he says. "After that I didn't worry anymore. I knew I was in God's care. Either I was going to be with Him, or I was going to rejoin my family."

On Saturday, fifty-six hours since David's accident, Missy was about to cross the bridge for the fifth time in three days, this time in her grandfather's car with her younger brother and mother.

"As we got closer to the bridge, she kept asking her grandpa to stop," says Becky. "She was very persuasive." Missy badgered her grandfather, crying and insisting that the truck was still stuck underneath the bridge. "Finally," Becky says, "we got about a half mile down the road and he told her, 'All right, I'm going to turn around and show you there isn't a truck underneath the bridge.'"

But the moment they pulled over next to the bridge and got out, they could see David's truck clearly. Becky went down to the embankment to the wreckage, to see if anyone was inside the pickup.

"I could see the truck and that there was somebody there," she recalls. "As I went down, I kept on saying, 'Sir, can you hear me?' He just never responded. And I got closer to the truck, he just looked up. And that's when I hollered at them on top of the bridge to go and get help."

David Miller arrived at the hospital with a broken nose, cracked ribs, and a collapsed lung. He had gone nearly three days and nights without food or water, all the time enduring excruciating pain. He believes it is a miracle that he's alive.

"If there wasn't a miracle from above, there is no way that I would be here," declares David.

It turned out that David's sons had driven over the bridge many times in their search. But only Missy, from her high seat in the bus, could see him.

Missy visited a heavily bandaged David in the hospital a few hours after his rescue. "He looked like he wanted to hug me and didn't want to let go. But he couldn't because he was still hurting," Missy remembers. "He kissed my hand, and called me his little guardian angel."

"When we pray to God, He's always listening," says Missy, "and if you believe, He will answer your prayers. I believed. And He answered mine."

TIFFANY'S WITNESS

SHELBY PHILLIPS

Believe on the Lord Jesus and you will be saved.

ACTS 16:31 NLT

"Bye, Mom!" Paul yelled as he ran out the door to meet his girlfriend, Tiffany Phillips, and some other friends. It was one of those spontaneous Sunday afternoons when the world belongs to those who grasp it—and today, that meant a group of five teenagers.

Just an hour earlier, Tiffany had joined Seaside Christian Church, wanting the world to know of her love for Jesus Christ. Her life had been good, with parents who loved her and cared for her. She excelled in track and volleyball, loved her friends and knew they loved her. But nothing could equal that moment when she trusted Christ as her Savior, knowing He gently held her life and heart in His hand.

Now she was off to celebrate that life with a group of friends as they headed for the Tillamook cheese factory to have ice cream and shop in the gift store. When they stopped to pick up two more friends, Tiffany unfastened her seat belt and slid into the middle of the backseat, next to Paul. Then they headed off down Highway 101, loudly singing songs from the movie *Grease*, not paying attention to the sporadic Oregon rain.

Rounding a slight curve moments later, the songs died as Jeremy, Tiffany's friend, lost control of the Subaru. They slid across the centerline, into the path of oncoming traffic. Jeremy automatically clutched the steering wheel and braced himself as a pickup hit them on their rear corner. The Subaru turned enough to clip the truck once again. Then, as they spun 360 degrees into more oncoming traffic, a van slammed into the Subaru's left side, crushing the three teenagers in the backseat.

Paul knew nothing else until medics strapped him onto a gurney. He didn't yet realize that in that moment of eternity, four lives changed and one life that truly had just begun had ended.

The next morning, students at Seaside High School returned to classes for the first day after Christmas break. They greeted each other across hallways, asking about Christmas presents and winter holiday fun. Some noticed the small, quiet huddles of students sprinkled in classrooms and halls. Some heard rumors, but couldn't quite believe the news.

Half an hour later, incredulous silence filled the school's halls. The principal had announced Tiffany's death and the injuries of the other four friends in the car with her. Everyone knew Tiffany. Some were in band with her. Others ran in track or played volleyball with her. Friends had walked with her to her parents' candy store downtown, even managing to get free samples on days they needed extra encouragement. Some had worked with her on Pacific Project, a senior year community project, putting together food baskets for needy people.

All of them had seen her smile, heard her encouraging words. "She was the first person I met who wasn't afraid to love anybody," student Josh Lively would later say.

Being the good kid she was, Tiffany's life had not changed drastically when she trusted Jesus Christ as her Savior at the Winter Youth Celebration. She simply decided at that point that everything she did would be for God's glory and purpose.

Tiffany was a girl who asked questions and would think through her decisions. A few months earlier, she had attended the Luis Palau Coastal Crusade with her boyfriend, Paul. "She sat in the front row at Youth Night and fully participated," Paul's mom said. "But she didn't go forward then."

Mike Hague and Terry O'Casey, youth and senior pastors at Seaside Christian Church, helped answer some of Tiffany's questions one evening. Still, she wasn't ready to publicly commit her life to Jesus Christ.

But at Winter Youth she was ready to give her life to God. On a Sunday morning, January fourth, she was ready to tell the rest of the world. Her mother sat in the church congregation, happy to see her daughter making her statement of faith. She couldn't have known how much it would mean to her in the few days that would follow.

Tiffany's public statement of trust in Jesus Christ quickly traveled beyond the church walls. The services of Seaside Christian Church were videotaped and broadcast on the local cable network. The high school showed the video every day the following week. All week long students filled the library to hear her testimony.

God continued to use Tiffany's life to touch others' lives. At Seaside Christian Church the next Sunday morning, her best friend Juliet and twelve more young adults walked the same aisle Tiffany had walked a week earlier. They, too, surrendered their lives to the gentle, loving hands of Jesus Christ.

THE LAST HURRAH

ZACH ARRINGTON

For wisdom is better than rubies; and all the things

that may be desired are not to be compared to it.

P R O V E R B S   8 : 1 1

It has come at last. There were several times when I doubted I
would survive to see it, but I did. I have fought the good fight,
run the long race, and beat the bad marmot to death. It is the
end of the year. People, one by one like little tributaries, are
trickling out of this place of higher education, going back to
their particular places of origin. Watching them leave, I suddenly
realize that I am going to miss them. For the past several
months, I have eaten, breathed, and studied with these people,
and I had become so wrapped up in everything that I hadn't
realized how much I genuinely like them.

My room is empty now. One of my roommates has gone,
taking the television with him. I sit and stare at the window. The
silly little posters and pictures that used to adorn the walls are

> "ENJOY
> THE LITTLE
> THINGS,
> FOR ONE
> DAY YOU
> MAY LOOK
> BACK AND
> REALIZE
> THEY WERE
> THE BIG
> THINGS."
> Robert Brault

now packed away, leaving the walls barren. I can't help but think back to the first time that I saw this room. The word that came to my mind when I saw it was *"cell."* But in a matter of months, the word *"cell"* had been replaced with the word *"home"* without any conscious thought.

The most turbulent year of my life has come and gone, and I haven't had time to notice. New things were thrust upon me with such swiftness and immediacy that the only thing I could do was accept them. Looking at the person I used to be and the person I have become makes me realize, beyond a doubt, that this year has changed me fundamentally. Survival has forced upon me the habits of responsibility, organization, and social graces.

The strength of the human species is to adapt, to survive. Those who are not up to the task of adapting are weeded out. It's not like college is going to take you in, make you into some corporate clone, and spit you back out. It will put you through the test. It will challenge what you are made of. But it will refine you, not destroy you.

I studied for all my finals in a daze. I was in a "finish-the-race" mode. I became a workaholic for a week and made sure I did everything right so I wouldn't have to go back and do it again. I laughed and talked and consorted with my friends, but all the while I was in the same state of mind that one has immediately after a car accident. After it happens, and you're safe and standing on the curb looking at your wrecked car, you think, *okay, what just happened here? I can't believe I just lived through that!*

I took stock of those I now consider close friends. Just months before, they had been total strangers. It's humbling to realize just how much our lives are shaped by "chance," or the infinite and intricate hand of God in which we all walk around.

My friends and I all gathered at Common Grounds, the local coffeehouse, to laugh and hug and say our good-byes. It wasn't a tearful occasion. We know that we are just taking a really long weekend. We'll see everyone on the flip side and have plenty of time to get sick of one another again. There were so many faces. I marveled at how close I had grown to these people without ever realizing it.

Friendship is a funny thing. By the time you reach college, it's not nearly as simple as it used to be to become a friend. Back in the good old days (kindergarten—where else?), if you wanted someone to be your best friend, you just asked, "Will you be my best friend?" You might have even offered your very best friendship in exchange for some kind of service, like being given the extra piece of candy from their lunch.

Through four years of high school, a small group of very close friends were the pillar of my existence. I found myself separated from them in college. I think my initial separation shock at the beginning cast a big dark cloud over the rest of the year. I felt so alienated it seemed I was always second-guessing myself.

The moral of the story is that if you can be yourself, and avoid worrying about fitting in and impressing people, you will find people who like you—that you enjoy as well. I spent too much time lamenting the fact that I didn't have any friends—when they were right there, staring me right in the face the entire time.

Right now the campus is filled with parents who have come to help their kids move back home for the summer. College leads to a drastic change in perspective when it comes to your parents. Instead of simply being seen as taskmasters, they become people. You begin to realize they have real emotions, rational reasons for doing things, and can even be funny at times—though not too often. (Ha ha, just kidding, Dad.)

I know your mom may have gone a little batty when you were preparing to leave, and she may get a little overeager for your return, but other than that, your relationship with your parents becomes pretty cool. You start to realize what spectacular people they must be to have put up with you for all your life.

I decided to give myself an extra day to pack instead of trying to get everything ready and rush home immediately. Plus, several of my friends were staying, and we decided to rent a movie. We felt like having a good laugh that night. Instead of renting a comedy, however, we did what may be the most fun thing you can do at a video store. We went through that entire mountain of tapes, looking for the absolute worst movie we could find. What we came up with was an intended psychological thriller, but it wound up making us laugh wholeheartedly.

That horrible, forgettable, stupid movie was the perfect way to leave. While watching it we had fun together. No matter how much I grow up, I never intend to lose the ability to have fun. All the riches, wisdom, morals, education, and achievements in the world do you no good if you don't enjoy it in the end—or in the process.

It seems that a lot of people think "becoming an adult" means you must set aside enjoyment of life and instead focus on success. Whether it's financial success or domestic success, you're supposed to be relentless in your climb to the top, at the expense of fun. I think that's a crime. I'm sure Jesus laughed a lot more than He cried. That's just not what we read about.

The world is full of excitement. Life can be full of joy and music and beauty. The fact that people can overlook it—stuns me. Seize every opportunity to laugh and to make others laugh. If you just look at the world around you with a fresh pair of eyes, you can't help but smile. There's so much hope and laughter to be realized out there. It's sitting out there right under the world's nose. Hardly anyone recognizes it, even though the world needs it so desperately. At the risk of sounding like a hopeless optimist (which I am), spread the light and pass the salt.

The car is loaded, filling every available square inch of space. The two open square inches I started out with on the trip up here have now shrunk to a quarter of an inch because of the stuff I purchased this year. I run up to the front desk and sign out, returning my key, and swing by my room for one last check before I head back home.

I go over the room one last time for anything I may have left behind. All the nooks, crannies, and corners have been cleaned out meticulously. It gives me sort of a shock when I realize that I am the one who did the cleaning. I never knew I was capable of this much organization! Everything looks to be in place.

I walk out of the room, pretending that I'm not ever going to look back. I get about three feet. The door hasn't even shut before I decide I must go back and have a last silent moment with the pathetic little box that has been my home. As I open the door, I am amazed at how untouched the room looks. Every trace of our existence has been removed. The chairs are face down on the desks, just as we were instructed to put them.

The bare walls gleam white; nothing of the personality we hung on them remains.

The first time I walked in this door and had this view, I was carrying an armful of stuff and preparing to start out on a new phase of my life. The sun of the afternoon bounced off the floor and spread around the room, illuminating it.

Though the room very much resembles that first entrance, I also realize how different I feel now. The person who first entered this room is not the same one now leaving. The room has not changed, occupant certainly has.

BOYFRIEND BETRAYAL

NANCY C. ANDERSON

(names have been changed)

For God has said, "I will never fail you.

I will never forsake you."

HEBREWS 13:5 NLT

I paced the floor and looked anxiously at the black-rimmed clock in the school cafeteria. I was waiting for my boyfriend, Jason. He was supposed to meet me for lunch, but he was late, as usual.

I went looking for him, and as I walked around the corner, near the Science Lab, I saw him. He was walking, hand in hand, with my best friend Jill!

She had the decency to look away in shame, but he looked me in the eye, smiled a cruel smile, and casually said, "Hi, Nance." They just kept walking. I fell against the wall as my knees and heart folded.

At first, I was numb to the pain, but soon the anger of the double betrayal began to simmer, and then boil.

I said aloud, "Jerks. Both of them!"

I went through the rest of my classes with a steeled determination not to cry. I made it all the way home. As I locked the door to my bedroom, I unlocked the door to my heart and the jagged tears bit my face. I cried until I was empty.

Jason had been my whole world. He was one of the most popular boys at school and, when I was with him, I felt important. I liked being defined as "Jason's girlfriend" partly because I hadn't developed any other definition.

I thought, *How could he betray me so easily? And with Jill!* She had been a close friend since seventh grade and I didn't understand how she could have done this cruel thing to me.

I thought my life was over. I felt like less than nothing.

I tried to pray, but I couldn't get my mouth to form any words. I picked up my Bible by the nightstand and held it to my chest as I simply said, *Help me, Jesus.* I felt better. Stronger. I opened it and read the verse in Hebrews 13:5 NKJV, "For He Himself has said, 'I will never leave you nor forsake you.'" Then I thought of the song we often sang at church, "On Christ the solid rock I stand, all other ground is sinking sand." I had been standing on Jason and he was crumbling away.

He broke my heart, but I knew that I would become stronger, with time.

In the next few months, I started to develop my own identity. I auditioned for a part in a play and was thrilled to get the part of "Townswoman #3." I didn't have any lines, but I was happy just to be part of the team.

I met many new friends and was even nice to Jill, even though she had one of the lead parts in the play.

I started to discover things about myself; hidden treasures. I took a creative writing class and I poured myself into it. I was the only one in the class to get an A+. I also volunteered to teach a children's Bible study, got involved in my church youth group, and took a part-time job at a restaurant.

A few months later, I learned a valuable lesson as I then watched Jason betray Jill and move on to the next victim.

I never again measured my worth by another person's loyalty to me. As I learned to trust God, and use the gifts He had given me, I saw that His love for me was consistent and unfailing. I knew that He would always be loyal to me and I would always be very valuable to Him.

I also learned that even though people will disappoint me and I will disappoint myself, God will never leave me or betray me.

BIG DREAMS & HARD LESSONS

APRIL STIER

**But seek first his kingdom and his righteousness,
and all these things will be given to you as well.**

MATTHEW 6:33 NIV

A cold, biting wind whipped my black skirt around my legs and tossed my hair into my face. A heavy silence permeated the air. I watched people of all ages gather around me. Streams of people came from every direction, but we all had the same destination and purpose. I was only one face among hundreds that came to honor the life of Jacob Charles Cushman on February 1, 2001, but I was one life that would be forever changed by his death.

With my arm tightly woven through my best friend's, I watched my brother walk on his crutches behind the rest of the pallbearers. The sight caused my heart to plunge in my chest. This could have been my brother's funeral. Fresh tears gathered in my eyes. I thanked God again for sparing my brother from this tragic car accident that left two of his close friends dead and another still fighting for his life in critical condition at the hospital.

My eyes searched for Jake's family. People crowded close around the tent to shield themselves from the piercing wind, and they blocked my gaze. As I looked up at the overcast sky, I could hear Jake's mom sobbing.

I was scared. During the past two years I had been struggling with my own dreams for the future. I had big dreams, and these dreams were precious to me. I didn't want to fail while trying to achieve them, so I had clutched them tightly in my grasp, too afraid to take the risk and attempt to chase them. Only in the past two weeks had I gained enough courage to finally pursue them, and now I was even more afraid thinking Jake's death had somehow proven that nothing is ever certain in life.

The pastor began to say a few words, but they scattered with the wind. I huddled next to my best friend to stay warm as I felt emotional numbness overtake my body. When the service ended, I walked in a daze to the car and mechanically climbed inside. I stared with bleak eyes at the mass of people scattering in dozens of directions. The ride back to the church was silent.

I buried my feelings during the potluck dinner at church after the funeral service and felt relieved when we finally left for home. Once at home, I didn't know what to do with myself. I was incredibly tired, and all I wanted to do was escape reality. I changed my clothes and fell into bed. Tears kept me company until exhaustion claimed me.

I woke up slowly. My body felt drugged, and my mind was cloudy. Memories quickly pounced on me, and grief wasn't far behind. The familiar heaviness settled back on my chest, and I pushed back the covers. Rubbing a hand over my face, I walked into our living room. Mom sat passively watching TV and informed me that Christopher was at the Cushman's house. Dad had gone to bed, and she was joining him shortly. It was still.

I walked back to my room. I couldn't go to bed; I had just gotten up from a nap. I'd never sleep through the whole night. *I could read.* I pushed that thought aside. I wasn't interested, and I knew my mind wouldn't stay focused. *Listen to music then.* I stuck a CD in my player. Sitting on my bed, I let my mind wade through the events of the day and finally faced everything.

Jake was dead at twenty years of age, I'd never see him again, laugh at his jokes again, or watch him play his guitar again.

Words from the funeral flooded back to me…my brother's speech about how Jake centered his life around what God wanted him to do…another girl saying it was Jake's greatest dream to see the face of God…someone mentioning that Jake's goal in life was to change the world's faulty philosophy.

Then it hit me. God was Jake's dream. Jesus was his goal. He lived his life completely for God, and now he was fully in God's presence. Understanding flooded my whole being. That day I chose to make God my dream. I laid all of my own hopes and desires at the foot of my Creator and said, *Take me, Jesus. All of me.*

I realized in that instant that to be a Christian did not mean merely to pay your dues to God through Christian service and then wait for God's approval in return. Following Jesus demanded *everything* from me—my very life. Only then would I know true happiness and experience the fullness of Christ.

Jake had understood that. Jake dreamed of changing the world's philosophy and the way we think. He changed my philosophy on life that very day. I still have my dreams, but now I am not afraid to chase them. Now I am not scared to see them possibly fail because God has become my ultimate dream. And He is one dream that I know will never fail. As long as I am where He wants me to be and doing what He wants me to do, then my dreams are attainable.

MY HOPE

DANICA ELMER

May your unfailing love rest upon us,
O Lord, even as we put our hope in you.

PSALM 33:22 NIV

"LOVE
MAKES
ALL HARD
HEARTS
GENTLE."

George Herbert

It was the first day of camp. I was excited, I was nervous, and I didn't know what to expect. But all my emotions did not prepare me for the week that was ahead.

As camper registration started, Heidi and I waited expectantly for our cabin of smiling girls to come waltzing into the cabin door, ready for an exciting week of camp. Heidi occupied the big "counselor" bed. I had a lower bunk as the "counselor-in-training." We sat twiddling our thumbs, waiting.

Our girls began to come in and set up their bunks, eventually filling the bottom bunks. Three girls were settled in, but there were still more to come. In walked Hope. "All the bottom bunks are taken," I commented, smiling. "You can choose from these other four top bunks." I heard a sigh, a sound of obvious displeasure, and I got a scowl. But Hope grudgingly filled a top bunk.

We continued to wait for the other expected campers while the sense of boredom in the room became overwhelming. Heidi and I tried to make conversation, but our four campers, who had never met, seemed to have been bitten by the shyness bug. All were very quiet and polite—all except Hope. Our simple questions were met with her snappy and sometimes snide remarks. "Is this going to be like boot camp?" Hope asked as we struggled to fill the silences. With the attitude of disgust she conveyed, it was apparent she did not want to be at camp. "No way! It's going to be a great week!" I responded, not knowing what a week it would turn out to be. My relationship with Hope had started.

We all started to feel more comfortable with each other by the time dinner rolled around. We trudged down to the dining hall where the plaza was crowded with expectant high schoolers. Dinner was the first scheduled activity for the campers, and I was excited for the week to start. Dinner was a little bumpy, but we got through the next hour without too much other trouble.

After dinner, with our stomachs full, Heidi and I gathered our four campers and headed to chapel. First, we built camp unity with team competitions and other fun activities. We also had a time of worship. But I noticed that Hope did not sing at all. The speaker was captivating, eye-opening, and challenging, yet I sensed Hope was far away.

In cabin groups after chapel, we talked about our lives and how we related to God. There was a wide spectrum of personalities in our cabin. We had four distinctly different campers with different needs, interests, and attitudes towards life. Heidi and I tried to be as open as we could about our own lives, hoping to encourage our campers to have genuine, real relationships with us and God. Overall, our small group of four girls responded well to our attempts to build such relationships. But when it was Hope's turn to share, she refused. At that point I knew that she was hurting, but I didn't realize how much. The burden and connection I felt to Hope were growing in my heart.

In the meantime, we kept Hope busy. I focused on Hope the first couple days of the week, and, in spite of herself, she began to "get into" camp. During one of the free times, Hope and I went on the zip line. We were harnessed in and snapped onto a cable, which extends from the top of a hill to the bottom. We then catapulted ourselves down, flying through the air with only a cable supporting us. During several other free times, Hope and I would play on the "blob," a huge balloon floating on the lake. Sometimes I would lie on one end and Hope would jump off the tower, sending me into flips until I landed in the lake. Other times I would take my turn flipping Hope.

There were times when I had to be her counselor authority, but slowly I began to see the shell of her negative attitude slipping off. As Hope began to feel more comfortable with her surroundings, I began to see her personality's potential. The Hope I began to see was a girl who could be extremely fun and talkative. The Hope I got to know while going down the zip line or jumping off the blob, was strong and daring. Despite my first impressions, Hope was becoming my friend.

The Hope that became my friend also became my concern. The Hope I wanted to get to know was hurting. The only way she knew how to heal was through acting out. Hope would continually complain about doing things she didn't want to do too. She was not about to be told what to do or how to do it.

There were things about Hope that annoyed me. She drove me crazy when she started to pluck her eyebrows and wouldn't stop. She worried me when she borrowed my sweatshirt and disappeared before chapel. She made me want to scream when she would ask me over and over if she had to bring her Bible to chapel.

But if there were things about Hope that annoyed me, they were overshadowed by the love that grew in my heart for her. I deeply wanted for Hope to know God. I wanted her to know

Him in the way that I do, as an intensely personal God who loved me and her enough to die for us. I wanted her to spend eternity with me. I had never prayed so long or sincerely for anyone else. I had a burden in my heart for her.

And each day, Hope began to open up little by little. Through snippets of conversation and simple interactions, I learned that something had happened which prompted her not to attend church or believe in God anymore. Her best friend had recently died in an accident, and she questioned God. Despite her apparent disinterest in spiritual things, I began to see a longing Hope didn't know how to handle, a hole in her heart she didn't know how to fill.

The week flew by, and as part of our evening cabin groups one night, my co-counselor, Heidi, shared how God had brought her out of a life of drugs and alcohol. That night, Hope asked to talk to me.

I was ecstatic that she trusted me enough to share with me. But at the same time I was really scared. I was worried she was going to tell me something awful. I had suspicions that her home life was tough. In the time leading up to our conversation, I prayed, asking God to give me words of wisdom.

The next morning, I pulled Hope aside, and we talked in a quiet stairwell. It was nothing earth-shattering or amazing; we simply talked about what she believed. She admitted she didn't know what she believed. We talked a little about her involvement in drugs and alcohol. And I explained to her the basics of the Christian faith.

I was struck by the fact that she had approached me rather than Heidi. I thought Heidi could have identified more with her situation and experiences than I. But I realized Heidi was not in the same position of trust I had created for myself with Hope.

So I continued to pray for Hope. As I did, her attitude began to slip away, and she became easier to hang around with. But my time with her was coming to a close, and Hope still hadn't made the decision I hoped she would: to follow Christ. I wanted that so desperately for her. I was also beginning to feel drained, both physically and emotionally. I decided to give my relationship with Hope to God. I knew that He wanted her to come to Him as badly as I did, but I realized He had His own timing. I also knew Hope had major hurdles to get over. But still, every time campers were invited to commit their lives to Christ, I prayed, *God, please!* and I would watch her response.

During our last night at camp, I knew Hope was running out of time. I watched her closely to see if there was any indication of a change. She gave no response. I was desperate for her salvation. I didn't have any more time.

Later that evening, when we were praying as a cabin group, Hope prayed for the first time all week. It was several simple lines, but its simplicity and the changes it was starting to represent brought tears to my eyes.

That prayer wasn't the only change that occurred that night. While waiting out in front of the chapel for the next activity, Hope leaned over to me and whispered quietly, "I prayed that prayer." That "prayer" was the prayer to follow Christ. There was nothing magical about that prayer, except for the change that should accompany it, but it was a start. I was so overwhelmed, I could barely hold it all in. I pulled Heidi aside into a room off the chapel and told her what Hope had just told me. And I sobbed. Sobbed because of my happiness, my relief, my tiredness, my love, and the realization that my relationship with this precious girl was causing change in her life. My hope was being realized.

Hope left that next morning with the other high schoolers I had come to know and love over that short week—but not before I was able to talk to her about her decision to become a Christian. I talked about what it really means to be a Christian. I told her I wanted her decision to be sincere. I explained to her what changes come as a result of the commitment she made. She had some tough situations to enter back into at home, and I wanted her decision to be real.

While I couldn't make Hope's decision real, the decisions and changes in my own life that week were real. I learned what it means to love someone unconditionally, in spite of their actions and reactions. I learned how to turn my life and situations over to my best friend, Jesus Christ, and how to talk to Him all the time. And I learned more about how a relationship with someone can change both parties involved.

And as a counselor, I saw as much of a change in me as I saw a change in the girl who walked in the door with a scowl and an attitude, and the same girl who hugged me when she left.

LIVING LIFE GOD'S WAY

After reading these true stories of people who experienced God's grace and power in their lives, perhaps you realize that you are at a point in your own life where you need special help from God.

Are you facing a temptation? A broken relationship? A major disappointment?

Are you ready to experience forgiveness and salvation? Encouragement and hope? Wisdom and inspiration? A miracle?

Though God's power and grace are deep and profound, receiving His help is as simple as ABC.

A—Ask: The only place to start is by asking God for help;

B—Believe: You must believe—have faith—that God can help you;

C—Confess: You must confess—admit—that you truly need God's help to receive it.

Living life God's way doesn't mean that all troubles disappear, but it does mean that there will always be Someone to turn to with all your needs. Call on Him now. For more information on how you can live God's way, visit our website at:

www.godswaybooks.com

RIGHTS AND PERMISSIONS

MEET THE CONTRIBUTORS

Nancy C. Anderson has been writing and speaking to women's groups for more than twenty years. She lives near the coastline in Southern California with her husband, Ron, and their teenage son, Nick. She can be contacted at *www.NancyCAnderson.com.*

Candy Arrington is a freelance author whose publishing credits include *Writer's Digest, Discipleship Journal, Christian Home & School, The Upper Room, Focus on the Family,* and *Spirit-Led Writer.* She is a contributor to *Stories for the Teen's Heart,* Vol. 3 and *Stories from a Soldier's Heart* (Multnomah). She coauthored *AFTERSHOCK: Help, Hope, and Healing in the Wake of Suicide* (Broadman & Holman Publishers, 2003). Candy lives in Spartanburg, South Carolina, with her husband, Jim, and their two teenage children, including Neely, who told this story.

Zach Arrington, a senior at Baylor University in Waco, Texas, and is the author of the book, *Confessions of a College Freshman.*

Esther M. Bailey is a freelance writer with more than eight hundred published credits. She is coauthor of two books: *Designed for Excellence* and *When Roosters Crow.* She resides in Phoenix, Arizona, with her husband, Ray. You can e-mail her at *baileywick@juno.com.*

Mike "Pinball" Clemons is coach of Toronto Argonauts of the Canadian Football League. He was the star running back during his 12 seasons playing for the Argonauts, breaking many team and league rushing records.

Cheryl Costello-Forshey is a poet whose work has been published in 16 books to date, including 11 books from the best-selling *Chicken Soup for the Soul* series, as well as the books, *Stories for a Teen's Heart, Stories for a Faithful Heart, Stories for a Teen's Heart 2, A Pleasant Place,* and *Serenity for a Woman's Heart.* Due to the countless number of requests that Cheryl has received, she has put together a collection of her poetry, which she soon hopes to have published. She can be reached at *costello-forshey@1st.net.*

T. Suzanne Eller is a prolific freelance writer and author of the book, *Real Teens, Real Life, Real Stories,* published by Honor Books.

Ken Freeman is author of *Rescued By the Cross: Stepping Out of Your Past and Into God's Purpose.*

Kelita Haverland is a country music recording artist from Canada.

Myra Langley Johnson has been writing for Christian publications since 1985. Her work has appeared in such publications as *The Lutheran, Today's Christian Woman, Standard,* and *Christ in Our Home.* She and her husband, Jack, attend Kinsmen Lutheran Church in Houston, Texas, and also volunteer with a therapeutic horseback riding program. They have two daughters and four grandsons.

Charlie "Tremendous" Jones began in the insurance industry at age 22 and built a $100 million business division over the next decade. The author of the classic best-seller, *Life Is Tremendous,* he has spoken and inspired millions of people worldwide over the past 25 years.

Lena Hunt Mabra, a freelance writer, recently retired from the field of Health and Wellness to spend time with family and pursue her writing full time. She is currently employed as a ghostwriter for a professional athlete and has an e-book and wellness program focusing on the balance of mind, body, and spirit for women.

Karen Majoris-Garrison is an award-winning author, whose stories appear in *Woman's World, Chicken Soup for the Soul,* and *God Allows U-Turns.* A wife and mother of two young children, Karen describes her family life as "Heaven on earth." You may reach her at: *innheaven@aol.com.*

Stefanie Morris has worked as a public relations professional in advertising and PR firms, nonprofits, and state government. She is actively involved in drama and children's ministries in her local church. She and her husband live in the countryside near Austin, Texas, with two dogs, two cats, four goats, one donkey, and roughly 100,000 honey bees! Her other hobbies include gardening and reading.

Kristi Powers is a full-time human development specialist—in other words, a Mommy! She resides in Wisconsin with her husband Michael and their two young sons, Caleb and Connor. Kristi has been writing stories about her life since she was a little girl, and loves to share from the heart about her relationship with God.

Michael T. Powers, a youth pastor, resides in Wisconsin with his wife Kristi. His stories appear in 16 different inspirational books and he is the author of the new book: *HeartTouchers.* For a sneak peek or to join the thousands of world-wide readers on his inspirational e-mail list, visit: *www.HeartTouchers.com.* Michael can be reached at: *Heart4Teens@aol.com.*

Tamekia Reece is a freelance writer residing in Houston, Texas. She enjoys reading, writing and giving advice. Her publishing credits include: *Chocolate for a Teen's Dreams, Insight Magazine,* and *College Bound* among others. She can be reached at *tekareece@yahoo.com.*

Tonya Ruiz is a popular speaker and the author of *Beauty Quest, A Model's Journey.* She lives in California with her husband and four teenagers. Visit her website at *www.beautyquest.com.*

Nanette Thorsen-Snipes is a freelance writer of 20 years and an award-winning author. She began writing in 1981 when her mother was terminally ill with cancer. She began with a year of humorous family columns in a local newspaper. She has always had an interest in writing, a strong desire was born at that time to write from her heart.

April Stier is a freelance writer from Indiana, who can be reached at *april_lynn03@hotmail.com.*

Christy Sterner is the *God's Way* series editorial consultant and has 10 years of experience in the Christian publishing industry. She has written for many series including *Hugs* and *Chicken Soup for the Soul.*

Gloria Cassity Stargel is an assignment writer for *GUIDEPOSTS* Magazine; a freelance writer; and author of *The Healing, One Family's Victorious Struggle With Cancer,* published originally by Tyndale House Publishers. *The Healing* has been re-released in special updated edition by Bright Morning Publications. Call 1-800-888-9529 or *Visitwww.brightmorning.com.*

Colleen Wheeler was a film actress when she experienced a dramatic conversion to Christ. She is now a part-time staff member at her church and attends Bible college where she is pursuing a degree in theology.

TELL US YOUR STORY

Can you recall a person's testimony or a time in your own life when God touched your heart in a profound way? Would your story encourage others to live God's Way?

Please share your story today, won't you? For Writer's Guidelines, future titles, and submission procedures, visit:

www.godswaybooks.com

Or send a postage-paid, self-addressed envelope to:

God's Way Editorial

6528 E. 101st Street, Suite 416

Tulsa, Oklahoma 74133-6754

This and other titles in the *God's Way* series
are available from your local bookstore.

God's Way for Fathers
God's Way for Mothers
God's Way for Teens
God's Way for Women

Visit our website at:
www.whitestonebooks.com

"...To him who overcomes I will give some of the hidden
manna to eat. And I will give him a white stone,
and on the stone a new name written which
no one knows except him who receives it."

REVELATION 2:17 NKJV

WHITE STONE BOOKS
LAKELAND, FLORIDA